Sacred Search for Sanity:

Spiritual Psychotherapy

ISBN 0-9716484-1-7
LCCN 2004099599

Sacred Search for Sanity:
Spiritual Psychotherapy

Linda Bearer Tuttle

Pathways of Lights
Santa Maria, CA

Acknowledgements

With my heart, mind, and soul I am grateful for the years of loving support, patience, and assistance from a most incredible man, my soul mate, my love, my friend, my husband Ed Tuttle. So many times throughout the years when my faith wavered, he would reach into the depths of my soul and shine the light of spirit. *"In truth, it is not for the love of a husband that a husband is dear, but for the love of the soul in the husband that a husband is dear."* [1]

There is a saying that we stand on the shoulders of all those who have gone before us. I stand now in appreciation of my mother and father, Ethel and Emery Bearer, who blessed me with a goodly heritage. My soul sings songs of gratitude to be so fortunate to have a mother who is also a friend.

And for Ruth MacQuiddy, a friend who is like a mother and a constant source of love and inspiration.

Dedication

To my Grandmother, Helen Ross, a shining star throughout my life. I guess when you told me I was "too damned old to go to school," what you meant was you wish I had started earlier so you could be here to see what I have done since then. I miss you.

Author's Note

From an early age two themes have directed my life path and actions: love and spirituality. My understanding of both evolved as I morphed from a Hopeless Romantic into a Hope-filled Healer.

There is a plethora of books and articles that teach and refine the nuances of theory and technique within psychotherapy, counseling, and other healing arts. Little has been shared about the impact of love and spirituality in the therapeutic process. Doing research on this subject has been personally fulfilling and rewarding. What struck me with amazing clarity was overwhelming evidence of the impact and power of love and spirituality in any relationship, but especially with healing encounters.

Continued work in this area brought new understanding and a realization that *love is spirituality* just as water is ice, a seed is a tree, and coal is a diamond. Time and effort are required in the maturation process.

Young love is motivated by self-interest and fantasy. When it matures and the spiritual component develops, the motivational emphasis shifts to understanding and acceptance, first with our intrapersonal relationship and then extending to interpersonal relationships. Some aspect of this maturation process is a central component in most therapeutic encounters. If a therapist has not done her work in this area, it will be difficult to help others find their way to individuation and interdependence.

When doing therapeutic work, it is not uncommon for the therapist to feel alone. It is not work that one can sit by the fireside and share with family and friends. To maintain a sense of balance and inspiration, a therapist must find ways to inspire and encourage himself to continue and to hold on to hope, even in the face of seeming defeat. To this end, it is my desire to share motivating ideas with therapists, counselors, teachers, ministers, and all others who are interested or involved in healing professions.

Table of Contents

INTRODUCTION

. . . some people have realized that the Inquisition is in the past, making it permissible and even healthy to question religious dogma and doctrine.

OFF-LIMITS

As a child it was drummed into many of us that "polite" people do not talk about sex, money, or religion. These areas were considered to be too deeply felt, too personal, and too strongly charged to be discussed in public. Therefore, individually and collectively, these subjects have all too often been treated like the third rail of a subway system. The third rail gives the electrical charge that provides the motive power. Touch it and you die.

Good or bad, over the past several decades, the shroud of secrecy has been partially removed from each of these sensitive subjects. Sex has moved from the privacy of the bedroom to prime-time television. Financial information is readily obtainable through Internet access. And some people have realized that the Inquisition is in the past, making it permissible and even healthy to question religious dogma and doctrine. So why are these subjects, which are the centerpieces in personal and relational difficulties, often off-limits in the therapy room?

Discussion on the subjects of sex and money must be postponed for another time and place. The importance of religion, or more specifically, the roots of religion, spirituality, and beliefs within the therapeutic process, will be examined. Engaging in the therapeutic process without reflecting on the impact of spirituality as a vital factor is challenging, if not impossible, to consider. It would be like cooking without fire, operating a computer without electricity, or sunbathing at night.

Edward Edinger provided insight to the principle function of psychotherapy by looking at the origin of the root words "psyche" and "therapeuein." He shared that psyche means "soul" or "life spirit"; [and] the Greek verb therapeuein means to "tend or render service . . . to the gods."[1] With this basic understanding, that the essence of psychotherapy is for the purpose of rendering service to the soul or life spirit of a person, it is the intention of this author to explore religious, scientific, and psychological materials while examining the extent to which psychological healing requires the care, attention, and treatment of the soul, the life spirit of a person. To look at the effectiveness of psychotherapy when it is considered a spiritual practice and when the transpersonal dimension is embraced. Also, to consider what happens when working in the invisible realm, must we be willing to acquaint ourselves with that which cannot be seen?

CHAPTER ONE

OVERVIEW

Healing is a process dedicated to the
ultimate goal of peace, a search for
sanity that occurs in the psyche and
encompasses every aspect of beingness.

Psychotherapy: Sacred or Profane?

Many people perceive that the essence of psychotherapy is problem solving. Is it possible that healing, the ultimate goal of psychotherapy, can be achieved by only working to resolve the issues brought to therapy by the client? Or does healing originate with the psyche, the principle of life. How did psychology, the study of the psyche, the soul, develop into a secular discipline? What makes a discipline sacred or profane other than the individuals who participate in it?

Anyone who has ever seriously engaged in psychotherapy understands the impact and implications of the term "soul-searching." Soul-searching is an adventure, an exploration of all areas of beingness: mental, physical, emotional, social, relational, and spiritual. If this idea is true, then it is inconceivable to explore the invisible inner world of an individual without examining the issues important to soul: faith, beliefs, and the values that underlie the ability to trust and to empathize. Diving into the depths of the unconscious, examining the intangible and ethereal, is a sacred—a spiritual—endeavor. When one appreciates this, it is difficult to understand the current definition from the *Merriam-Webster Collegiate Dictionary* that psychology is "the science of mind and behavior."[1]

This limited definition leaves one with more questions than answers. What mind, and where is it located? Is it simply a function of the brain? It appears not. The idea that mind is not limited to the brain has been explored by many philosophers, psychologists, theologians, and scientists. In the *Holographic Universe*, Talbot's work supports the idea that the activity of mind is found everywhere in the body.[2] A popular PBS documentary with Bill Moyer on the mind/body connection examined numerous research projects that all support the premise that mind is not limited to the brain.

Beyond the mind/body connection is the tenet that mind is a quality, an activity that is both local and non-local, both personal and universal. This is not a new belief. Ralph Waldo Emerson wrote, "There is one mind, common to

17

all individual men. Every man is an inlet to the same [mind] and to all of the same [mind]."[3]

Moving to the science of behavior—is behavior simply reactions and responses to one's environment or is it a product of mind? What impact does the inter-play of emotions, instincts, and intuition have on behavior? Too many questions are left unanswered by those who embrace Webster's stark and narrow perspective—an over-simplistic view that acknowledges only the tip of the iceberg and results in a therapy that works only with the most easily observable aspects of an individual.

Those aspects which lie beneath the surface in the depths of the individual, in the soul of the person, are the root causes that bring someone into the presence of a psychotherapist. If psychology relates only to the brain and behavior, it loses its original essence, the breath, life, and soul of its beginnings. True healing requires more than the surface adjustment of behavior, or the unraveling of the most prominent mental states of the patient. Healing is a process dedicated to the ultimate goal of peace, a search for sanity that occurs in the psyche and encompasses every aspect of beingness.

When a therapist and patient meet, it is essential that they are devoted to their work and that they treat it with reverence and respect. In *Psychotherapy and Spirit,* Cortwright emphasizes this when he wrote, "Healing, wholeness, integration, cohesion, or health depends upon reconnecting the ego to its deeper source."[4] Understanding this, how could therapeutic work not be considered as sacred?

Evolution of Psyche

The concept of psyche or soul within psychology is not defined nor bound by any religious creed or dogma; it is infinite and universal. It transcends the soul-concept held by man-made religions. When spiritual needs go unmet, or are thwarted by organized religion, the need to ask deeper questions is spurred. During a lecture in 1997, Dennis Slattery, director of the Mythology, Literature, and Religion department at Pacifica Graduate Institute, in a lecture emphasized this idea by saying, "When religion no longer serves us, the psyche will develop." The evolution and growth process of the human psyche has given birth to psychology, to the search and study of the soul. Even the Bible acknowledges this movement of consciousness: when "deep calls to deep," Deep answers (Psalm 42:7).[5]

The psyche is mystical in its depth and breadth; it is universal, yet it is individualized in each person. The individualized soul seems to forever be searching for a connection to the larger dimension of itself. This human quest yearns to gain more knowledge and understanding of where humanity came from, where we belong in that overall scheme, what is the meaning of that relationship, and how can we survive in the interaction with the universal and continue to maintain ourselves as individual entities.

The scenario of self-seeking-Self has many faces and is played out on many levels. It can be seen when individuals interact with religion, with psychology, and with other people. The arena in which this drama is experienced will determine its name. Whether it is known as a spiritual journey, a search for God; a psychological quest, a search for Self; or a dynamic interpersonal relationship, a search for Other or Thou, it is all a search for Wholeness.

Consider the words "wholeness" or "wholly." They contain the concept of being complete, lacking in nothing, which explains their relationship to the word holy. Hence, wholeness is related to that which is holy or sacred. In addition, the word health comes from the root word heal, which has its origins in the word wholeness. With this in mind, the word sanity, meaning good mental health, can be directly related to the idea of wholeness. Whether one considers this search for wholeness, or sanity, as a transpersonal or interpersonal journey, it is not difficult to see that the individual is looking for more of who they are, and how they can belong and best function in the world with a larger perspective of Self.

The disciplines that are most involved in providing opportunities for individuals to focus on transpersonal and interpersonal searches are religion and psychology. In August of 1996, the *American Psychological Association Monitor* dedicated its publication to psychology and religion. It reviewed the similarities of how both were founded in belief systems, traditions, and the use of rituals. The articles explored how both disciplines focus on right, wrong, guilt, and what it means to be human. It emphasized how both help people find meaning and purpose, and how to cope with life. The cover article suggested that the biggest difference between the traditional Christian religions and psychology is the tendency for religion to put the responsibility for an individual's life in the hands of God; whereas psychology stresses the significance of personal responsibility. This is a debatable statement since one of the primary goals within therapy is to help the patients gain a sense of connectedness, which is not limited to their relationships with other people unless the therapist or client is limited to that perspective.

Another reason for being open to the spiritual in therapy is explained by Anne Gottlieb, Ph.D., who said, "Once you take the psyche out of psychotherapy, it's more appropriate to call it behavioral health care."[6] Behavior is only a part of the whole; it is the external manifestation of an internal state. Psychology is so much more than the study of behavior. In *The Religious Function of the Psyche*, Lionel Corbett states that "any experience that touches on questions of meaning, value, or purpose is potentially religious . . . any process which explores such questions with a transpersonal perspective becomes a religious process, including psychotherapy."[7]

Many Faces of Love

There is yet another reason why psychology and spirituality appear to be inseparable disciplines. Not only do they both respond to questions about the meaning of life and assist people in a search for wholeness, but both disciplines are based in a quest to understand the healing power and human need for empathic attunement. To be empathically attuned to another person is to experience the deepest meaning of love and compassion.

Due to the basic limitations of the English language, it is difficult to grasp the immense impact of love in the therapy room. Just saying "love in the therapy room" leads to a variety of misperceptions and the budding of potential innuendoes. Normally, the use of the word love in a religious or spiritual context is far more acceptable. There is even a word, *agape*, which has been created to describe a Christian love, a universal love, lacking in lust. Somehow the words empathic attunement or transference/ countertransference, which were created to describe the intense and special therapeutic relationship, seem to lack passion. They also have little meaning or acceptance outside of the psychological community. Even within psychological circles there is considerable disagreement over the meanings of these parochial phrases.

Therefore, we seem to be stuck with the use of the word love, which is a small, symbolic representation of an incredibly important, monumental, dynamic process that is essential for a healing environment. This importance is unveiled in the essay "Modern Christianity and Healing," when Kelsey states, "There is more communication in love than any intellectual process."[8] Sincere communication can take place without words, but it can never occur without love. Love is the unseen, but palpable presence in any healing relationship. Love is often unspoken, but can always be heard. In love's unchanging steadfastness, there is transformative power.

Larry Dossey, a physician who has dedicated much of his life to research on the healing power of prayer says, "Love occupies a majestic place in healing. Lying outside space and time, it is a living tissue of reality, a bond that unites us all."[9]   In *Healers on Healing*, an anthology of essays written by well-known non-traditional healers, the editors, Carlson and Shield, commented that they gathered the writings to search for a common denominator for all healers and healing methods.[10]   Many of the practices presented in the book were drastically different from each other.   However, the one golden thread that was addressed by every healer, and which ran through each healing method, was love.

Additional insight is added to the idea of love as the binding "living tissue of reality" in Paul Fleishman's *The Healing Zone: Religious Issues in Psychotherapy.*   He wrote, "As I understand it, human love is not *in* any person, because by definition it is about that which opens, connects, and transcends bridges. Love belongs to the between."[11] Love cannot be given out for healing by a therapist or minister, as a doctor or pharmacist might dispense medication for physical healing. However, Fleishman suggests that they can "hold steady in the possibility of its emergence."[11] When a therapist manages to maintain a space that is safe for her patient to experience the seed of love, she is aware of the feeling and recognition of a mutual blessing. What can be more sacred than this?

Mutual Blessing

Too often the idea of therapy as a mutual blessing is overlooked by both therapists and patients. Generally, therapy is a misunderstood process. The most commonly held idea is that the patient will come to therapy and the counselor will "fix" them or at least help them to see what is causing the problem, and make suggestions about how to improve the situation. Thinking of therapy as a fix-it situation is an incomplete and erroneous view.

The primary process that happens in the therapy room affects both the patient and the therapist. In Murray Stein's book *Transformation,* he clearly wrote that the relationship between the therapist and the patient "becomes a dynamic factor that changes both people in the direction of a mutual image of integration and wholeness."[12] The wholeness that Stein referred to is further explained by Jung's statement that "Wholeness is a combination of I and you, and these show themselves to be parts of a transcendent unity."[13]

There are few experiences that compare to being present during a healing encounter. The blessing the patient receives as he heals is more apparent. Healing begins when patients learn it is safe to share their deepest fear, anger, resentment, guilt, shame, or other hidden negative emotions. Release happens when old wounds are open, wounds that have often lain festering beneath the surface for years, like pockets of emotional puss holding past injuries of abuse, neglect, indifference, or serious misunderstandings. Once shared, the patients learn that their burdens are made lighter, the pressure less, and negative emotions are neutralized in the atmosphere of acceptance.

The blessing for the therapist is as complex as the healing process. Being privy to another's secret inner world offers burdens and blessings. The responsibilities are legion, and yet they offer tremendous opportunities to gain deep understanding and appreciation for the resilience of the human spirit, the value of trust, and the power of acceptance. There is an indescribable exchange of energy that grows exponentially and goes beyond the people in the room. These are some of the blessings that keep those in the healing professions returning to their work.

The blessings are sometimes so subtle that they go unnoticed. During a recent session, I met with a young woman who was struggling with anxiety and a desire to make changes in her life. She was tormented by the dilemma she created and the demons of anxiety. She brought a dream to the session, and after working with it, she discovered that her unconscious had some clear preference for how to proceed. Her anxiety decreased and the change was obvious in her entire demeanor. Those were some of her blessings.

My blessings included seeing her less tortured and finding hope. But an unexpected blessing happened as we worked on her dream. I saw within the dream symbolism something that helped me with a totally different type of situation than the one she was working on.

We both left the encounter with a deeper understanding of how the unconscious is always offering assistance. We had new insights into our lives and ideas about how to progress on our separate life paths. Both of us were energized and filled with hope. We were truly mutually blessed. The fact that she brought something to her session that was helpful to me is one of the many unexpected blessings I have received from therapy sessions. It is like a Christmas bonus that happens intermittently all year long.

Invitation to Wholeness

A special kind of "magic" takes place in therapeutic encounters where the numinous is invited, even expected to be part of the process. This does not mean that there is a conscious or verbalized invitation. The invitation is established in the mental, emotional, and physical atmosphere of the therapist, and when possible, in the room prior to the patient arriving. Ann Belford Ulanov in *The Functioning Transcendent* stated that "the Transcendent functions in our lives all the time, whatever we choose to call it—God, or the unknown, or the holy, or the numinous, or the all-in-all. When we take notice of this reality, it responds by showing us how it functions in us."[14]

Cooperating with the Transcendent allows an individual to relax in relationships, recognizing that his primary job is to be fully present. Carl Jung seemed to understand this when he noted that "there are spiritual processes of transformation in the psyche."[15] If every moment is considered to be sacred, then everyone and everything that enters into that atmosphere will be seen as having spiritual potential, an opportunity for healing. The acknowledgment of possibilities opens the door for transformations to take place.

If in doubt, watch the most profound change, as seen in the simplest of activities. In the reverie of a walk, immerse yourself in thoughts of joy; feel and appreciate the wonder and beauty of the Universe that surrounds you. Look at nature's vast supply showing itself in the colorful splashes of budding flowers, the differing shades of green grass, and the multitude and types of trees. As you are savoring nature's many blessings, take note of strangers who are passing by. Look into the eyes of the faces where life has left stress and sadness. Smile, shower a sense of peace, plant a seed of happiness, and take note of how often the seed takes root and produces an immediate change in a thirsty and hungry soul. In doing this simple but, oh, so powerful exercise, you will have engaged in sacred work. You will have entered into the realm of spiritual encounters, and you will know in the deepest recess of your being that something special has taken place.

A similar dynamic takes place when a therapist and/or a patient bring the transcendent consciousness with them into therapy. One does not have to be smiling like a Cheshire cat or be ecstatically happy to feel and to share the additional power and peacefulness that transcendent consciousness brings to each encounter. William James shared that healthy-minded souls realize the presence of God in the soul and the universe by "opening of the eyes of the soul in which Reality is bathed. For them the earth is literally 'crammed with heaven'."[16]

When someone approaches any situation with a spiritual perspective, he is likely to maintain a calmer demeanor. Even when that person is confronted with traumatic events and other negative happenings, he is not as likely to be drawn into the drama of the emotional chaos. For therapists, this means that they can know and hold the belief and the image of wholeness for a patient, even when the patient is only able to experience empty, negative, depressed, or lonely feelings. When a therapist knows that the opposites, faith, hope and love, are available for the person she is with, she is able to be fully present, and listen without feeling anxious or pressured to fix the patient.

Therapists who come from a spiritual dimension are able to watch their patients engage in their sacred search for sanity, for the wholeness, in somewhat the same manner that parents watch their children playing hide-and-seek. They may give the searcher clues, but they know even in the face of fear, frustration, or anger that there is great joy awaiting those who are able to accomplish the discovery without being shown or told. A therapist is often compared to being a wise parent. What wise parent does not pray that he will provide sufficient opportunities for his child to mature physically, mentally, emotionally, and spiritually?

The emphasis on the importance of spirituality has grown rapidly over the past ten years. Every area of life seems to have received a wake-up call regarding the spiritual dimension. A paradigm shift is taking place as people become increasingly aware of a vital need for spirituality. This shift is pushing spirituality back into its home, in the field of psychology.

Psychology grew from the roots of religion and philosophy, and then moved into the house of science. It is time for the family to be reunified, for psychology, spirituality and science to come back together, to embrace, and to learn from each other.

As a sign that this is beginning to happen, the *DSM IV*[17] committee recognized that religious and spiritual problems are important enough to be given a diagnosis, and created a category for them within the V Codes. The American Psychological Association has published a book, *A Spiritual Strategy for Counseling and Psychotherapy*, which opens with this quote from Teilhard deChardin: "We are not human beings having a spiritual experience; we are spiritual beings having a human experience."[18]

The time has come to acknowledge the psyche in psychology. From the depths of the soul of psychology a cry can be heard for the sacred search for sanity. Just as good parents do not ignore the needs of their children, when "deep calls to deep," Deep will answer. It is time to listen.

Body and mind and Spirit, all combine
To make the creature, human and divine.
Of this great Trinity, no part deny.
Affirm, affirm, the great eternal I.
Affirm the body, beautiful and whole,
The earth expression of immortal soul.
Affirm, affirm the mind, the messenger of
the hour,
To speed between thee and the Source of
Power.
Affirm, affirm the Spirit, the eternal I--
Of this great Trinity, no part deny.
Ella Wheeler Wilcox[19]

CHAPTER TWO

DEEP CALLS
UNTO DEEP

The tension created by soul seeking spirit gives rise to the eternal inexplicable questions of "Who am I?" and "Why am I here?"

Give Me Meaning

All through the history of mankind, there has been an ongoing search for the meaning and purpose of life. For a while I had a message on my answering machine that said, "This is not an answering machine, it is a question machine. The questions are: Who are you and what do you want? If you have trouble answering these questions, don't feel bad. People throughout the ages have had the same problem. After the tone, why don't you give it a try?" The reactions and responses were varied, including one person who wanted me to change it because they had given my name to a prospective employer and did not want that person to think they had a "weird reference."

The idea of giving callers something meaningful to think about was enjoyable. Eventually, I changed it because many people found it intimidating. To be clear about whom we are and what we want, or what our desires and purpose in life might be, requires that one has spent time soul-searching, a mysterious and sometimes daunting activity. Faced with that challenge, many people prefer to turn on the television, call a friend, or climb in their cars and use the radio to drown out any questions or meaningful communication that may be trying to get through from their soul or the transpersonal dimension.

One might find that surprising in the light of Joan Borysenko's comment,

> The nourishment and growth of the soul is the very reason for human life. When we nourish the soul we nourish God, increasing the abundance of the life that we can see . . . and the levels of the life that we don't see at all. In a larger sense, soul is the substance of the universe, knowing itself and growing itself.[1]

The soul she refers to is the individual manifestation of the impersonal Universal, Transpersonal, Spirit, God.

What's in a Name?

I hesitate using the word God, because attached to such a familiar word is an enormous variety of learned concepts and images, dogma and outright superstition, that are ultimately so subjective as to defy any possible single agreed-upon definition. Attempting to bracket, that is, to set aside those ideas in order to allow new ones to form is, at best, difficult. The need to shift from the concept of God learned early in one's life was considered so important to Jung that he thought no one over 35 years of age could heal without changing his religious outlook, his beliefs about God.[2] He said that there were times when he actually had to tell a patient, "Your picture of God or your idea of immortality is atrophied, consequently, your psychic metabolism is out of gear."[3]

The problem created by many Western religions is a belief in a God that is a being. A God who is separate and apart from humans, an anthropomorphic figure of a wise old man residing somewhere in the sky who inflicts pleasure or pain from a celestial seat of judgment. This is an image of God made in the image of man. When exploring the meaning of God, Jung indicated that he perceived God more as a deeply satisfying experience.[4] Jung explained this when he wrote, "High mountains, the rivers, lakes, trees, flowers, and animals better exemplify the essence of God," than the meanness, vanity, and egotism of men.[5]

Jung often referred to God as Self and shared that it was the part of a person that was compelled to find meaning from everyday life. On "Face-to-Face," during a BBC interview with him when he was eighty-one years old, Jung stressed that "Man cannot stand a meaningless life."[6] The need to find meaning and purpose in life seems to be seeded in the heart of man, and it is central to the thought of many great leaders in the fields of religion, philosophy, science, and psychology.

Sacred Search

One psychologist known for his work on meaning is Victor Frankl. His views can be explored in *Man in Search of Meaning* [7], his personal, powerful account about survival in a Nazi concentration camp. He is the originator of logotherapy, an existential approach that focuses on helping others to understand the meaning present in their lives. Frankl's work is important in the evolution of psychology, for it demonstrates that a person can withstand and cope with the most brutal, degrading, life-threatening circumstances, and find meaning in the midst of his suffering. [8]

Jung's work was also based on the human need to find meaning. Frankl and Jung both felt that the search for meaning was a sacred search, a spiritual quest. They would applaud Sam Keen's statement that "the search for spirit, for God, is ultimately the quest to know ourselves in our heights and depths. . . . It was, is, and always will be the greatest human adventure." [9] Let no one mistake this for an easy quest. Part of the joy, excitement, and thrill is that spirit is elusive and mysterious. Jung likened it to "very rarefied air" that can only be seen on old coins after working its magic on the copper.[10]

The very thing that lives within and without, that drives one to seek meaning in life, is impossible to see, except in viewing the products of its work. Attempting to see "It" would be like a fish in water, looking for water. We find its essence in the experience of soul moments. Marion Woodman describes them as soulful times:

> . . . when we see a magnificent sunrise, hear the call of a loon, see the wrinkles in our mother's hands, or smell the sweetness of a baby. During these moments, our body, as well as our brain, resonates as we experience the glory of being a human being.[11]

When these contacts with spirit are made, there is a connection that, like leaven in bread, travels to all levels of beingness. Our physical senses come alive with sight, sound, taste, smell, and touch. The mind keenly stands in total, though silent, awareness. The soul is filled with emotion, knowing it has embraced its kin, Spirit. There is a mutual harmonizing of being physically alive, mentally alert, and soulfully aware. There is an opening up to something "more." Maybe that is why "Spirituality is defined as the subjective engagement with a fourth, transcendent dimension of human experience beyond time, space, and language that enhances human life and evokes corresponding behavior."[12] When the spiritual dimension is consciously brought into an environment by one person, everyone around him benefits.

Spirit's Child

Should soul and spirit be viewed as interchangeable? In the article "Spirit: Resource for Healing," Rachel Naomi Remen, a physician and counselor, wrote that it is more difficult to say what spirit is not, than to say what it is. These are the things that are not spirit, even though they are often confused with, and may be the effects of, spirit: morality, ethics, psychic power, religion. Spirit does not judge, separate, sense, nor is it limited. She goes on to say that spirit is an "essential need of human nature, the elusive essence of life."[13]

On a transpersonal level, spirit can be likened to psyche, whereas "the soul (or anima) is the factor which relates the person to his or her inner world."[14] Jung specifically says that "it has the dignity of an entity endowed with, and conscious of, a relationship to Deity."[15] Soul is the personalized counterpart to spirit.

In working to understand soul and spirit, Jon Kabat-Zinn, a popular author on matters of soul and spirituality, notes that there is a difference between soul work and the movement of spirit. He states that "*soul work* . . . involves a downward movement in the psyche. . . . Soul can have a lot of heat and pain associated with it," which is different from the "movement of *spirit* which has a quality of moving toward the light—upward, ascending."[16] Both are seeking the other.

Perhaps soul and spirit are the underlying causal factors in the concept of enantiodromia, which was explained by Jung:

> Every psychological extreme secretly contains its own opposite or stands in some sort of intimate and essential relation to it. Indeed, it is from the tension that it derives its peculiar dynamism. There is no hallowed custom that cannot on occasion turn into its opposite, and the more extreme a position is, the more easily may we expect an enantiodromia, a conversion of something into its opposite.[17]

The human race will forever be seeking to understand and give meaning to this ongoing struggle.

The tension created by soul seeking spirit gives rise to the eternal inexplicable questions of "Who am I?" and "Why am I here?" Most likely, we will never know the full answer. Dr. Remen says that life may be for the purpose of "advancing some spiritual agenda that we all work towards together, without even knowing. There is a lot of mystery here. Perhaps life is sacred."[18] Knowing that, it is not surprising that the questions are not limited to individual pursuits, but the quest for meaning is felt within and across disciplines.

CHAPTER THREE

WHOLENESS
REVOLUTION

Although the disciplines of religion, science, and psychology tried to segregate the spirit, body, and mind of humans, they were not successful.

Conscious Evolution

In antiquity, everything to do with the spirit, soul, sacred, psyche, mind, and healing was embedded in religion.[1] Then as science gained insights into bodily functions and germs and medicine, healing was snatched from the cradle of religion and placed in the hands of the scientists. Philosophers grabbed onto the mind to secure its rightful place with the intellectuals. The heart was left untended, except when it was able to agree with some religious doctrine. Is it possible that it was the cry of human hearts, tired of their interrelated parts being separated and compartmentalized, that eventually caught the attention of sensitive souls like Jung?

Throughout Jung's life he was exposed to religion, since it was his father's profession. In *Memories, Dreams, and Reflections*, he speaks of the battle he experienced with his childhood concepts of God. Growing up, he made it an avocation to study religions around the world. He found systems of belief that recognized a person as a wholeness. Feeling strongly about his discovery, he said, "Just as the Creator is whole, so His creature, His son, ought to be whole. Nothing can take away from the concept of divine wholeness."[2] Jung's focus was to help people recognize that they are

. . . indispensable for the completion of creation; that, in fact, [humans are] the second creator of the world. The spirit within mankind has given to the world its objective existence. Without it life would be a meaningless series of endless days of unheard, unseen, silently eating, nodding heads birthing and dying through hundreds of millions of years. This numbing existence would have gone on into the profoundest night of non-being down to its unknown end. Human consciousness created objective existence and meaning, and found an indispensable place in the great process of being.[3]

Jung's beliefs were thought by many Christians to be blasphemous, and some still find them objectionable. Jung knew that many people would stand aghast at the idea of accepting the mantle of divinity. That is why he broached most of his writings in carefully chosen phrasing and verbiage that differed from the normal religious terminology. Albert Einstein could have been speaking to Carl Jung and all the great minds that were not afraid to entertain new ideas when he said, "Great spirits have always encountered violent opposition from mediocre minds."[4]

Jung recognized that the consciousness of man was evolving. He thought that the "life had gone out of the churches," and said, ". . . the next dwelling place the Holy Spirit appears to have selected [is] the human individual."[5] I would expound upon this idea and say that there is a wake up call from deep within the human soul to recognize that God, Life, the Holy Spirit, does not exist in any specific place or building. The Holy Spirit, when thought of as the Whole Spirit, allows one to envision that it is not restricted or limited to any place, space, or time. Jung heard the call from the Whole Spirit and he said, ". . . the Holy Spirit's task and charge [is] to reconcile and reunite the opposites in the human individual through a special development of the human soul."[6]

I think Jung would be pleased to know that many of the churches have moved past the exclusive concept that God only dwells in sacred settings. At the same time that Jung found himself disenchanted with traditional religious rhetoric, there were a few brave-hearted and thoughtful theologians who sought a larger concept of God. New Thought churches that consider themselves to be centers of "spiritual psychology" embrace Jung's philosophy. Like Jung, they introduced and integrated Eastern religious philosophy into Judeo-Christian belief systems. They were the first religious voice in the United States to suggest that God is Wholeness, everywhere present, including within individuals.

A message given by Ernest Holmes, one of the originators in the New Thought movement, founder of Science of Mind, sounds much like Jung:

There is a gradual awakening in the human consciousness, a concept of itself which is transcendent of the objective form. Every individual who lives can find that great within of himself which is immersed in God, and is of God.[7]

This idea that God resides in, through, and as human beings, that seemed so outrageous only a few years ago, is now considered to be an acceptable belief by most of the mainstream religions. It must be Spirit at work, seeding the human soul.

Warfare to Romance

The other major realization that comes along with the idea of wholeness is that although the disciplines of religion, science, and psychology tried to segregate the spirit, body, and mind of humans, they were not successful. Until recently, most Western religions had been "anti-body, seeking to attain spiritual liberation at the expense of the body and earthly life."[8] Over the past twenty years "the old warfare between science and religion has ended, and a new romance has begun."[9]

Psychology is the child of the uneasy union of science and religion, of the secular and the spiritual. Any wise approach to bringing about the revelation of wholeness in the suffering individual must include, embrace, both. It has not always been thus. Science, until the advent of quantum physics, wished to have nothing to do with the invisible realm, and denied its existence. Like the rebelling adolescent, it wanted nothing whatever to do with the orientation of the parent who embraced the presence of unseen forces as the causative factor in life. Science was convinced that if one could only determine and isolate the parts of anything, one could unearth the secret of its existence. Even poets were caught up in this idea:

FLOWER IN A CRANNIED WALL
Flower in a crannied wall,
I pluck you out of the crannies,
I hold you here, root and all, in my hand,
Little flower--but if I could understand
What you are, root and all, and all in all,
I should know what God and man is.
Alfred, Lord Tennyson[10]

As with all of life, there is presented here a paradox. Holding the flower, one does hold the evidence of the mystery in one's hand. But one cannot begin to know the "all in all," by considering the flower, "root and all," separate from the Wholeness of the source of its being, both visible and invisible. Examination of the part is valuable; it leads to specialization in any field. And it is valuable in the field of psychology; but any approach to the healing of the individual that confines itself to just the body, or just the mind, or just the behavior, or just to plumbing the unconscious, is incomplete. Psychotherapy requires cognizance of the entire individual, body, mind and soul.

Chapter Four

No Boundaries

The therapist cannot help but share his
consciousness with each client.

Universal Force

Irving Oyle was one of the first modern physicians to study and promote the importance of the mind, body, and spirit connection. He quoted Carl Jung as saying that "healing comes only from what leads the patient beyond himself and beyond his entanglement with ego."[1] In *Body of Knowledge*, Robert Marrone evaluates the body/mind/spirit connection in relationship to psychology. He suggests that "a psychology of personal and transpersonal healing begins with the lived-body—and the embodied experience of being related to a factor greater than the individual ego."[2]

Anthropological studies have repeatedly uncovered information indicating that every society and culture has within it a belief in something larger than any individual, some universal force that is even grander than the society itself. Marrone was adamant in declaring a need for psychology to acknowledge the wholeness, the transpersonal, and the spiritual aspects of a person's being. To split off mind, body, or behavior without consideration for spirit will maintain the "destructiveness of fragmenting factors that were destined to alienate us from each other, to make prisons of our bodies and psychic traps of our minds."[4]

Seamless Reality

Quantum physics and neuroscience opened the door for physical proof of the interrelatedness of the visible and invisible, the conscious and unconscious, the observer and observed. The research of the renowned physicist, David Bohm, points to everything in the universe as a "seamless extension." He explains that "it is as meaningless to view the universe as composed of 'parts,' as it is to view the different geysers in a fountain as separate from the water out of which they flow."[5]

A reality of cosmic oneness and unity with all life is a vision held by the mystics. Perhaps this is one of the reasons Jung was considered by some to be a mystic. Jung's concept of the collective unconscious is in direct alignment with Bohm's theory of the universe as a giant hologram. Both men, from very different disciplines, came to the same conclusion—that all things are interconnected. This being so, "Despite appearances, we are beings without borders," or as Bohm describes it, "Deep down the consciousness of mankind is one."[6] This speaks to the ability for thoughts and ideas to be shared without the need for verbal or physical contact and communication.

The oneness—the unity—is that which we are at a transpersonal level. Truly, within the essence of life is a spirituality that goes beyond the boundaries of religion. Einstein was aware of this when he wrote,

The most beautiful emotion we can experience is the mystical. It is the sower of all true art and science. He to whom this emotion is a stranger . . . is as good as dead. To know that what is impenetrable to us really exists, manifests itself as the highest wisdom and the most radiant beauty . . . this knowledge, this feeling, is at the center to true religiousness. In this sense . . . I belong to the ranks of the devoutly religious men. [6]

From this perspective, there is no doubt that there is a deep, genuine need for spirituality, which explains why there is such an outcry to seek a deeper and more meaningful understanding and connection than was previously available.

Prior to deciding to adopt the new diagnostic category of "Religious or Spiritual Problem" in the *DSM IV*, mental health professionals evaluated the therapeutic need for such a diagnosis. Surveys completed by APA-member psychologists reported that 60% to 72% of their patients addressed issues of a religious or spiritual nature. In their research, Lukoff, Lu, and Turner (1998) examined cases in the PsychInfo data bank. They found only 100 cases that referred to religious or spiritual problems. Of these, the most frequent issues that brought people to a point of "spiritual crisis" were when people experienced a loss of faith or were faced with a serious or terminal illness.

I have found that it is common for someone to question or lose faith whenever life presents undesirable situations. Many people will seek therapy for those circumstances that they find troubling, but fail to address the underlying confrontation with their faith and/or belief system. Therapists need to be aware and understand that people facing these issues are most likely also challenged on a spiritual level. Apparently this is not happening, since the survey of therapists revealed that only 29% thought religious issues were important in the treatment of their patients (Lukoff, Lu, & Turner, 1998).

The inclusion of the new diagnostic category in the *DSM IV* is one more way that the voice of spirit is going to be heard. Ernest Holmes predicted the call from spirit,

From the dawn of human history until today this inner awareness has produced a steady and unbroken sequence of accomplishment and progress, and while there have been periods when this evolution appeared to stop or to be broken, it has always started fresh and new. . . . The natural order of evolution has brought us to a place where there is a quickening of the spirit, a keener perception of the mind, a deeper introspection of the soul; the veil between spirit and matter is thinning. We are emerging into a spiritual Universe, proclaimed alike by the philosopher, the religionist, the scientist, and the idealist, and yet the nature of Reality or ultimate Truth cannot have changed. The awakening is to the mind and spirit, and from this mental and spiritual awakening follows objective equivalents.[6]

The time has come. Evolution has brought us to a point where people around the world are hearing the call from the Deep.

Outburst of Soul

Bill Moyer, a distinguished television commentator, has delivered information about religion, mythology, the human spirit, and the mind/body/spirit connection to the living rooms of the American public. Why has he chosen this area of specialization? He explains: "Any journalist worth his or her own salt knows the real story today is to define what it means to be spiritual. This is the biggest story—not only of the decade but of the century."[7]

The wake-up call is also noted by looking at some of the most popular books for the past ten years. There is a plethora of material exploring, musing, investigating, entertaining, and questioning concepts of religion, spirit, spirituality, soul, sacredness, and expanded reality. They are too numerous to begin to name. Jung predicted the explosion of consciousness in the sixties, saying, "The biological and political history of man is an elaborate repetition. History of mind is different—consciousness intervenes."[8]

What might happen if one refuses to listen to the call of Spirit, isolating her heart, mind, and soul from the current trend? Thomas Moore thinks that "when soul is neglected, it doesn't just go away; it appears symptomatically in obsessions, addictions, violence, and the loss of meaning."[9] Around the world, souls seem to be yelling back at Spirit's call with an outburst of the behaviors mentioned by Moore.

Carl Jung told a story about a trip he took to Africa. He required the assistance of natives to carry his belongings. On the third morning of the journey he was perplexed when the natives were not preparing to leave. He approached the guide in hopes of getting the natives to move on. He was told, "Three days we travel, now we must allow our souls to catch up."

Reading this story I was amused at thinking about what the natives' reactions would be to our current culture. How much might be gained if we allowed time for our souls to catch up? Would the world be a kinder and gentler place? Would we continue to face the troubles and trials that confront us personally and globally?

Soul Force

Since therapists are frequently confronted with patients who are struggling with problems, how can they respond in a way that will allow their patients to begin to heal? Some philosophers see human problems and negative behaviors as physical reactions to the feeling of not being connected to the oneness, to Spirit. The more violent the act, the deeper is the feeling of disconnection. In Martin Luther King's "I Have a Dream" speech, he states, "We must rise to the majestic heights of meeting physical force with soul force."[10] What is true on the streets of our neighborhoods is equally true in the counseling office.

No matter what theoretical approach or intervention technique is used to work with a patient, there is a need for a therapist to remember that what is in need of healing is the patient's psyche. Healing is accomplished by the patient gaining a sense of connectedness. The therapist can promote this process by nourishing patients at a soul level through kindness, compassion, thoughtfulness, and love.

Robert Sardello speaks to this saying, "Seeing the essence of soul as love, and love as more than emotion, desire, or sentiment, allows us to venture further than ever imagined into soul life."[11] When one engages in psychotherapy from a transpersonal perspective, the primary task is not so much what one does, as who one is and what one thinks.

A sacred search for sanity is "experiential at its core. It is only the experience of spirit that satisfies the soul's quest, and only by plunging into the depths of the inner heart and feeling can the realms of spiritual being be plumbed."[12] Jung understood that the quest for psychological growth overlaps the spiritual journey toward higher consciousness. According to Jung's protégé, Marie-Louise Von-Franz, therapy should lead to

. . . an experience of the Self, the inner wholeness that cannot be understood intellectually, but only through love. Jung writes, 'This love is not transference, and it is no ordinary friendship or sympathy. It is more primitive, more primeval and more spiritual than anything we can describe.' In this realm, it is no longer two individuals relating with each other on the personal level, but the "many, including yourself and anybody whose heart you touch." There, ". . . there is no distance, but immediate presence. It is an eternal secret . . . "[13]

The therapist cannot help but share his consciousness with each client.

When therapists are aware of the wondrous quality of the psyche through their own spiritual and psychological work, they bring recognition of the sacredness of psychological work to each session. They are acutely aware of their interconnectedness with each patient, and they will experience the marvelous interplay between the mental, emotional, physical, and spiritual realms. They will know that there is a source of help and power available to them and their patients that would otherwise be ignored and left untapped.

CHAPTER FIVE

SEEDS OF LOVE

Possibly, the concept of prayer, like the concepts of spirituality and sacredness, needs to be revamped.

You Want Me To Do What?

Although many may consider the thought of using prayer to be an unusual adjunct to therapy, if one is conscious of the unconscious connection, it seems important to keep one's thoughts about a patient as clear of pathology as possible. Prayer seems an excellent way to send "seeds" of love and wholeness out to a patient. Possibly the concept of prayer, like the concepts of spirituality and sacredness, needs to be revamped.

The following words of Ernest Holmes may begin to stir the lost truth about prayer:

Prayer is an inward and an outward movement, and since consciousness cannot separate itself from itself. . . [it is] a movement of consciousness upon itself. The calm moments of quiet contemplation when the soul beholds itself, and knows what it is and why it is, are brief compared to those of active life, and it is their purpose to shed the light of Spirit on the commonplace things of everyday life. A man should not desire to spend his lifetime praying, but should rather seek to make his work a prayer, his life a song, his living an art, his believing a certain knowledge.[1]

Our very thoughts are like prayers that leave our consciousness and go adrift in the collective unconscious, and therefore, can be heard by others at an unconscious level. What would you have the people in your life hear about themselves? As a therapist, what would want your patients to hear about themselves?

Larry Dossey, a physician who did extensive research on prayer, wrote *Healing Words: The Power of Prayer and the Practice of Medicine.* He suggests that prayer helps to quiet the mind, makes us aware of our thoughts, and is the equivalent of attention training. This is much needed since our minds have a habit of "wandering wildly—likened by St. Teresa of Avila to riding a bucking horse."[3]

Dossey was amazed to find in the research that praying for another person was proven to be effective, even when the two people were far away from each other. Prayer knew no boundaries even when the object being prayed for was in a lead-lined room, which shields its contents from every known form of electromagnetic energy. Prayer is unstoppable. Dossey found that the most powerful prayer is not when specific results are requested, but when an attitude of prayerfulness was engaged. Prayerfulness is regarded as the attitude and feeling of empathy, caring, and compassion.

Long before any research on prayer was even considered, Ralph Waldo Emerson knew the importance of this approach. He said,

Prayer that craves a particular commodity—anything less than all good, is vicious. Prayer is the contemplation of the facts of life from the highest point of view. It is the soliloquy of a beholding and jubilant soul. It is the spirit of God pronouncing his works good. But prayer, as a means to affect a private end, is theft and meanness. It supposes dualism and not unity in nature and consciousness. As soon as the man is at one with God, he will not beg. He will then see prayer in all action. The prayer of a farmer kneeling in his field to weed it, the prayer of the rower kneeling with the stroke of his oar, are true prayers heard throughout nature.[3]

This type of prayerfulness points to our ability to hold a vision of wholeness for ourselves and others. To recognize that

the same life force lives in all—the burst of energy that opens flower petals is the same energy that creates stars. It is the same energy that comes out of the blue to inspire, excite, and delight us with gifts of understanding, compassion, and reassurance.[4]

When we can hold this type of thought for those who are struggling to gain a new vision of themselves and their lives, then we are truly embracing a spiritual psychology.

After Larry Dossey found the scientific evidence supporting the effectiveness of prayer, he had to ask himself, as a scientific doctor, "Are you going to follow these scientific directions and actually use prayer?" He went on to say, "Over time I decided that not to employ prayer . . . was the equivalent of deliberately withholding a potent drug or surgical procedure."[5] For months after his decision, Dossey grappled with finding a prayer ritual that he found satisfying. He finally settled on going to his office early, entering a meditative state, and asking only that "Thy will be done" for each of his patients. He never did research on the result of his personal prayers, and shared that he doesn't know the specific results. He feels that they were effective "if for no other reason than I felt more connected with those I served."[6] What could be more important for a therapist?

Healing - Not Curing

Friedrich Heiler, a noted theologian who made a life study of prayer, says, "A prayer is the expression of a primitive impulsion to a richer, intenser life . . . . It is always a great longing for life, for a more potent, a purer, a more blessed life." Later he declares, "The effort to fortify, to reinforce, to enhance one's life [or the life of someone else] is the motive behind all prayer."[7]

However, regardless of how good one's intentions are, a therapist should heed Jesus' comments about prayer. "When you pray, go away by yourself, all alone, and shut the door behind you" (Matthew 6:6). To espouse personal beliefs would be a shameful use of therapeutic authority. Being spiritual is not about sharing religious concepts and ideas, nor sharing prayer. It is about being prayerful, being spiritual, and living from a sense of authenticity, compassion, and love.

The other point which has already been partially addressed is to remember that prayer is not about affirming an outcome that meets with our approval. It is not for the therapist to decide what might "cure" another person. Jung expressed concern that "there is a widespread prejudice that analysis is something like a "cure," to which one submits for a time and is then discharged healed."[8] Wendell Beane, the former chair of the Department of Religious Studies and Anthropology at the University of Wisconsin, also cautions that "Curing has the nature of fixing." Curing, the "fixing" of symptoms, is much different from healing. Beane saw healing as "the restoring of equilibrium in the otherwise strained relationship between a person, fellow human beings, the environment, and God. This process includes physical, emotional, social, and spiritual dimensions."[12]

The therapeutic focus should never be on a cure. The outcome is for the patient to decide, not the therapist. The heart of therapy is working in the present moment, which is the healing process. Therapy is the witnessing of patients as they journey toward health, toward an ever-increasing ability to function more fully in the three major areas of life: love, work, and play. From a spiritual perspective, the therapist sees the patient as learning about the essence of wholeness.

All the experiences in life are part of the process of wholeness. After working with people who are dying and learning about near-death-experiences, Rachel Naomi Remen realized the central themes regarding the purpose of life. She says, "The purpose of life is to grow in wisdom and to learn to love better. If life serves these purposes, then health serves these purposes and illness serves them as well, because illness is part of life."[10]

CHAPTER SIX

TENDING THE CARE
OF SOUL

Although pain may be written in the
mind and displayed in behavior, I believe
it catches its first breath and lives on in
the depths of the soul.

Pathway to Healing

Walk into any hospital emergency room and with one look at the tortured faces, the sight of blood, accompanied by heart-breaking cries of anguish, you will know that you are in the presence of trauma. Nurses, doctors, and hospital staff rush to care for the patients' immediate needs. They work to stabilize patients and to provide the support needed for them to survive. A traumatized patient is not so easily detected in the counseling office. Psychological trauma is not so readily seen, often overlooked, and frequently misdiagnosed. Just as high blood pressure is known as the silent killer, psychological trauma should be recognized as the unexpressed emotional slayer. Symptoms which indicate that someone is traumatized often go unacknowledged, even by the individual who is suffering.

Psychological trauma is challenging to diagnose because not everyone responds in the same way to stressful, disturbing, and shocking life events. What traumatizes one person may have a very brief and limited negative effect on someone else, and may in fact energize resources within them that they had not previously been aware of. Therefore, if the traumatized person does not engage in an emotional tirade or total withdrawal, that person's need for assistance may go unnoticed.

Physical trauma and psychological trauma also differ in the equipment and procedures required for treatment. When one compares a doctor's office, with all the equipment, to a typical counseling office, the difference is readily apparent. The contrasts between the two offices speak volumes about the dissimilarities in treatment approaches.

Treatment of psychological trauma is as subtle as the non-intrusive, sensory-pleasing counselor's office, and as enigmatic as a person who looks and acts strong and healthy, but inside is dying emotionally. The psychological treatment of patients suffering from emotional trauma can be incredibly simple, as in the three-step recovery plan outlined in Judith Herman's *Trauma and Recovery*: 1) Establish safety, 2) Work through remembrance and mourning, and 3) Reconnection.[1] Paradoxically, the work is not simple, it is bewildering due to the complexity of the human psyche.

The contemplation of human complexity and the wonder of individual uniqueness were instrumental in compelling me to study the dynamics of the healing art of psychology. To gain insight about what a person may need to promote healing, it seems eminently important to first understand the origins of that person's psychic pain. Although pain may be written in the mind and displayed in behavior, I believe it catches its first breath and lives on in the depths of the soul. The therapist's job is to gain entrance to the soul through the doorways of pain which are found in his patient's mind and behaviors. Although a therapist may enter a patient's private world initially by considering and evaluating the visible manifestation of behaviors, the real work of addressing mental and emotional pain takes place in the invisible, in the interrelated realm of mind and spirit—in the psyche or soul.

For years I have worked as a behaviorist and am a believer in, and advocate of, the principles used in Applied Behavior Analysis. After seeing many well-constructed behavior programs fail, I wondered what was happening. Observing carefully, as any good behaviorist does, I saw the same program result in success when used by one person, while another individual, appearing to implement the same program with the same person, failed miserably. The difference was not discernible—it was as if some individuals possessed a magical quality or force that allowed them to perform miracles with clients who had difficulty changing their behaviors.

The differences were so subtle that they were rarely seen, but there was a sense about what was happening. At times it could be observed in what seemed to be the most insignificant mannerisms. I once heard that more than 90% of communication is nonverbal. I would say a good part of the 90% is also nonphysical. What someone is thinking and feeling about another speaks volumes and manifests in responses to that which is neither seen nor heard.

When therapists are truly nonjudgmental and accepting, they possess a key to unlock the barriers and open the way to healing. That is the reason therapists are constantly being told to work on their own issues so the past resentments and judgments do not interfere in the healing dynamic. It doesn't matter what methodology a therapist uses, the success of all therapies—behavioral, cognitive, psycho-dynamic, humanistic, existential, RET, eclectic, or integrative—will be limited by the therapist's ability to find common ground in the invisible realm.

Working in the Invisible Realm

As mentioned earlier, recent research, has demonstrated that the physical, mental, emotional, and spiritual aspects of a person are interconnected. One cannot do something that affects just one aspect of beingness without the other areas of life experiencing the ramifications. Like a hanging mobile assembly, change one element, the balance shifts, and the entire mobile is altered. When working in the realm of the invisible, it is even more obvious that it is impossible to address the mind or emotional state of a person without involving the patient's belief system.

In Cortright's work, *Psychotherapy and Spirit,* he expounds on the necessity for the spiritual dimension to be part of therapeutic work: "Transpersonal psychotherapy alerts us to the limitation and dangers of purely psychological approaches to inner states, cut off from spiritual traditions. For the spiritual traditions caution that everything a person opens to inwardly is not just strictly psychological."[2] Psychological healing requires the care, attention, and treatment of the soul, the life spirit of a person. Therefore, to achieve maximum effectiveness, psychotherapy should be considered a spiritual practice, one which embraces a transpersonal dimension.

Path with a Heart

When the pain experienced in mind and/or spirit grows too great to deny or ignore, an individual will often be driven by his pain to seek help, to begin the journey in hope of finding a path with a heart. This painful state of mind is aptly described in the Bible: "Why are you cast down, O my soul, and why are you disquieted within me?" (Psalm 42:11) The individual's choice to seek relief through spiritual or secular healing is dependent on his belief structure. Whether he goes to a minister, practitioner, or therapist, he will carry with him foundational beliefs, beliefs which are held at the deepest and most fundamental level of his being, beliefs which will have a profound effect on his ability to heal.

Jesus of Nazareth, a master psychologist in his own right, was fully aware of the impact one's beliefs had on one's openness to healing. He often offered a question like, "What do you want me to do for you?" (Matthew 20:32, Mark 11:36), or he would say, "Do you believe that I am able to do this?" (Matthew 10:28) Having established this foundation, this willingness to be healed, and the acceptance that he, Jesus, was the one to bring it about, healing took place. Then, immediately upon the person being healed, he would tell them, "Your faith (belief) has made you well." (Matthew 8:13, 9:22, 16:28, Mark 5:36, Luke 7:50)

This same faith and belief directs people today to seek out someone who they "believe" can relieve their suffering. This faith may be invested in a religious leader, a therapist, counselor, doctor, practitioner, teacher, friend, family member, or another human being who is believed to be able to fulfill the second half of the healing relationship equation. The reference to Jesus is not presented to set apart a particular religion, but to point to a principle, a dynamic, a spiritual dimension that is present in all such healing encounters. To function as a healer and not be aware of the importance of this dynamic in the therapeutic encounter, not to actively seek its presence, is to enter the relationship only partially prepared.

In our society where much of life is experienced in a fast forward mode, the therapy room seems to have replaced the nurturing atmospheres of the front porch and kitchen. The hearts of many yearn for the time when people would sit outside in the dusk of day and share their inner-most thoughts and concerns, especially the unwanted ones that invaded their peace of mind. When the chill of winter winds moved people from evening reveries on the front porch to the warmth of the kitchen, the conversations continued there. The kitchen, the hearth, is seen as the soul of the home, for much more than food is provided when friends and family gather around a table.

The soul feels abandoned by the current trend of family members eating in front of televisions. There is a sense of the loss of community with our loved ones and neighbors, a loss of the warmth and camaraderie. There is a tendency for people to share food and drink and hours of being together in the same house, yet all the while their hearts and minds and souls are left homeless. Many people today feel unconnected in these homes where the goddess Hestia no longer visits the hearth.

The therapist who creates a welcoming and caring environment is addressing this chronic need for a loving, open, compassionate,

91

and safe place for the troubled soul to begin to feel the connection and trust that is so critical to any successful therapeutic effort. It can be very much like finding a long sought after feeling of being "home." There is great peace in finding a place where someone will truly listen, a place where someone is willing to accept and be with one who is suffering, without judging. Finding such a place is an instrumental part of the healing process.

There is little doubt that a healing environment is also a loving environment. Not a possessive, romantic, or passionate love, but a soulful love, a transpersonal love that recognizes the spiritual dimension of the encounter. Transpersonal psychologist, Frances Vaughan, discusses spirituality, love, and the problems created in our society by the deep need for a more meaningful life, a need to experience spirituality and universal love. One quote in particular struck me as especially meaningful:

Spirituality is closely associated with the experience of universal love, which can be a powerful healing force . . . . In a world that has devalued the sacred quest, many people who long for unconditional love are eager to submit to someone who seems to offer it, and who takes on the role and authority of a parent. Such surrender can easily become an avoidance of self-responsibility. The desire to be as a child, free from the anxiety of not having answers to existential questions, trusting in a powerful, wise parent who offers guidance and protection, can be very compelling.[3]

The challenge of clarifying and working through issues surrounding the process of love and the many faces of love is something that every therapist needs to do. Many of the problems that patients bring to therapy will be about this puzzling and much coveted experience. The lack of loving experience lies at the root of much of the psychic pain which motivates someone to seek help. Even when relationship issues and concerns about love are not consciously brought into the therapy room, they are present at an unconscious level. Many times, feelings of love, or feelings about a lack of love, are projected onto the therapist. The importance of love cannot be over-emphasized, for as Erich Fromm said, "Love is the only satisfactory answer to the problem of human existence."[4]

No one should underestimate the power of love, especially a spiritual love, which often is referred to as the most powerful force in the universe. In *Healers on Healing*, a number of professionals in the healing arts, physicians, philosophers, metaphysicians, and spiritual teachers, share their ideas about healing. Throughout the book, it is obvious that regardless of the discipline, there is a common denominator or "golden thread" woven into all healing experiences. The golden thread is love. On the loom of caring, and the needle of communication, the golden thread of love can be woven into a person's life and a pattern of healing can replace a gaping wound in the psyche.

Charlotte Sophia Kasl opens *A Home for the Heart* with the following lines that exemplify and illuminate the essence and power of love:

Love is the energy at the center of all life. It is the reality beneath our fears, the breath, the seed of all that grows. Loving ourselves, loving others, and loving spirit/God are inseparable, for all life is interconnected and sacred. Love is an energy force like the air you breathe; if you withdraw your love from anyone, you take your breath away. [5]

Therapists can provide an emotional CPR, reviving and giving their patients new opportunities to choose life, by sharing a "breath" of life, the energy force of love. Remembering that the focus and originating purpose of psychotherapy is to tend to the soul, the life spirit of a patient, the significance of therapy as a loving and spiritual act cannot be over-stated.

When a therapist recognizes the importance and the power of seeing the therapeutic encounter as a sacred encounter, then everything about it changes and becomes more meaningful. Even when the patient is not consciously aware of the therapist's propensity to honor the sacredness of their meeting, the patient will feel the subtle differences. The honesty and openness and safety will speak through everything, including the physical environment. Love can take away the fears and allow someone to go where he has never gone before. Listen to how Rumi's words express the possibilities:

Love has a bunch of keys
Under its arm.
Come, open the doors.[6]

CHAPTER SEVEN

SACRED SPACE

Like fish in water, we are often not aware of the ocean of energy, in which we live and move and have our being, without which we would not exist.

Something Special

When the term "space" is used, especially in connection to a relational encounter, there is a tendency to automatically think about a physical area where people meet, or the distance that exists between them. Consider for a moment that the preeminent element of space is not empirical, but is ethereal and experiential. Conceptualizing space in this non-material dimension creates an awareness of a sense and feeling, a mental and emotional atmosphere. Within this dimension is a feeling of acceptance that arises from an unspoken, but very real heart-speak space present in the therapeutic encounter. It is out of this dimension of the physical space—the colors, lighting, furniture, wall decorations, and other objects of the meeting place—that the ambiance should emerge. The therapist can maximize the effectiveness of the therapeutic encounter by creating a physical space that honors her work.

All space is filled with energy. Like fish in water, we are often not aware of the ocean of energy in which we live and move and have our being without which we would not exist. Yet there are times when we consciously or unconsciously become aware of the energy in a particular place which is radiated by ourselves or another. Who has not experienced the pall of gloom and despair that seems to hover about a person in the throes of depression, or the effervescence of one caught up in some totally consuming enthusiasm over an idea or a project? Almost everyone has had the experience of walking into a room and automatically feeling uplifted and nurtured by "something," but not really being able to fully comprehend exactly what there is about a place that makes one feel good. It is sometimes, but not always, easier to know when something does not feel right, to be aware of what is offensive, disagreeable, or even dangerous.

Something about this Place

If you close your eyes and allow yourself to slip into a memory of some place that is special to you, you will in the present moment re-experience those feelings . . . feelings of love, joy, peace, happiness, and well-being. What is it about this special place that you have chosen that is so powerful that its memory carries nurturing for your psyche? Most people find their special place somewhere in nature, be it on a mountain top or in a meadow, in a valley or next to an ocean, lake, or river, or in a quiet grove of sun-kissed trees. It is rare for someone to envision a favorite place, a place that feeds one's psyche, to be inside a man-made structure.

Yet, if someone is asked to envision a sacred place, that person's mind normally goes to a religious structure, pointing to the idea that thoughts of sacred and/or spiritual are often assumed to mean something religious. In reality, sacred and spiritual are very different from something religious, even though they are frequently intermingled and often confused with each other.

Religions are man-made cultural organizations created for the purpose of encouraging spiritual growth through the adherence to a particular theological view or dogma. But spirituality belongs to the individual. Another difference lies in the basic meaning of the two words and the concepts behind them. The root word of religion means to tie or to bind, whereas, spirituality is about being unfettered, being freed. Sam Keen explains in *Hymns to an Unknown God* that "spirit, our capacity to transcend our familiar and cultural conditioning, has no gender, no nationality, no class, no color, no race."[1]

Frances Vaughan outlined the impact of spirituality within psychology, saying that "psychologically healthy spirituality is based on experience rather than dogma, and it respects individual rights and different forms of worship."[2] Vaughan then lists the characteristics that represent psychological and spiritual healthiness: authenticity, letting go of the past, facing our fears, insight and forgiveness, love and compassion, community, awareness, peace, and liberation. These soulful attributes are present in a sacred space and are as palpable as the furnishings in a therapist's office. Actually, the furnishings set the stage. They can be part of the expression that speaks to all who enter, "There is something wonderful about this place; it has the feeling of a sacred space."

A Sacred Place

So how does a therapist go about making his office a sacred place? Certainly, the answer is not to bring in religious artifacts that speak to exclusivity. Nor is it necessary to bring in an office design specialist. Even working in a place where no one has a specific office, small changes can be made that whisper to all who enter that there is something special, something sacred about this place. A major clue is contained in the meaning of the word sacred: "dedicated or set apart" and "entitled to reverence and respect."[3] The second clue is found in nature, where a person's mind goes to find peace.

When a place is respected, it is clean, without the feeling of it having been sanitized and reeking of artificial "fresh scents." It looks as if someone cares about its appearance. It often takes no more than a few minutes to look around a room to see what may need attention, in the same way one looks in the mirror for a last minute evaluation. The time invested in preparing a room will be well rewarded, for it radiates to all who enter that someone in this environment cares.

Karen Kingston, author of *Creating Sacred Space with Feng Shui,* invites her readers to look around them and "realize that what you are looking at is the outer manifestation of your inner self. Everything in your outer life—especially your home environment—mirrors your inner self."[4] This applies equally to the home away from home, the office. Kingston specifically refers to the therapy room, saying,

I worked for many years as a therapist, and I came to realize that no therapist can heal another person. People can only heal themselves. But what a therapist can do is create a very safe space for people to do their own healing in, channel universal energy for their benefit, and use their particular skills and talents to support them through their healing process. . . . Space Clearing your therapy room regularly creates a sacred place for your clients to feel really safe and let go on a very deep level. This produces much better results for them . . . [5]

Although "Space Clearing" is a specific technique that Kingston developed after studying similar processes used in cultures around the world, it begins with the simplest activities. She suggests that just cleaning and clearing away clutter will produce profound changes, as well as, repositioning furniture until it "feels" right. This may sound overly simplistic, but everyone is aware of how differently they feel when their home is clean, in comparison to when it is not clean.

While working at a nonprofit agency, I engaged in the act of Space Clearing, at first making small, seemingly insignificant, changes by clearing away unwanted items left by previous employees and items which were only used occasionally. Before inviting a new patient in, I checked to make sure the room was neat and tidy. I got permission to move furniture and pictures to places that opened up space and offered a sense of welcome. I brought in plants and fresh flowers to invite the energy of nature into the office.

These small acts were powerful enough in their impact to have the other employees and patients commenting that something was "different, more peaceful, better." There were no major renovations, just some nurturing acts for the space in which I worked. All the acts were in honor of the work that was to take place in this space and in an attempt to create a sacred place where people who entered felt a sense of serenity and safety.

CHAPTER EIGHT

SAFE PLACE

To help someone find his way out of
the darkness, a therapist must know
how to hold on to the light of hope.

Connection

In learning the art of therapy, one of the first lessons that are driven into the budding therapist's psyche, is the importance of creating a "safe container" for the patient. No work can be done when the patient does not feel protected. On the physical plane, a safe container requires the therapist to provide a place that is private, so the patient can speak freely without concern of being overheard. The mental and emotional levels, which are even more important, are more complex. One primary factor is that the patient must feel assured that the therapist will maintain her confidentiality. From that foundation, the therapist can build the relationship, establishing a sense of trust, honesty, and empathic attunement.

Every patient has a need to feel understood and accepted, to feel as if her soul is being nurtured, fed, and cared for by the therapist. In *Care of the Soul*, Thomas Moore outlines and describes this process. He wrote,

Care of the soul . . . goes beyond the secular mythology of the self and recovers a sense of the sacredness of each life. This sacred quality is . . . the unfathomable mystery that is the very seed and heart of each individual . . . . Care of the soul . . . appreciates the mystery of human suffering and does not offer the illusion of a problem free life. It sees every fall into ignorance and confusion as an opportunity to discover that the beast residing at the center of the labyrinth is also an angel. The uniqueness of a person is made up of the insane and the twisted as much as it is of the rational and normal. To approach this paradoxical point of tension where adjustment and abnormality meet is to move closer to the realization of our mystery-filled, star-born nature.[1]

Patients can only reach such a point, and learn to appreciate the beauty and power that resides within them, when they feel totally secure in being able to explore the labyrinth of their being, and reveal the "beast."

Most patients arrive at a therapist's door with a sense of helplessness and loss at their ability to trust themselves and others. The world no longer feels like a safe place to be. Judith Herman says that when a person's "sense of self has been shattered," it can be "rebuilt only as it was built initially, in connection with others."[2] In *Trauma and Recovery*, Herman outlines the establishment of safety as the first stage of trauma therapy. Is there anyone who enters therapy who does not feel the need for safety?

Whether they admit to it or not, people need to feel safe before they can allow themselves to be vulnerable, to open up, and to begin to trust a therapist. Gaining a sense of safety is more difficult for some people than others. The degree of vulnerability was clearly accented by Judith Herman when she said, "Survivors feel unsafe in their bodies."[3]

People who have been living in a home where traumatic events have occurred are often unaware that their homes have become like war zones. Consider for a moment what it would be like to have no safe place to go. No place to go for respite or peace. Living through traumatic situations can often leave someone with a sense that no safety exists—within or without. What a devastating thought, that there would be no escape from feeling insecure, no safe place to exist. Until his physical, mental, and emotional states are under some control, there is no way the person can begin to relate and interact with other people in a meaningful encounter.

These feelings could apply to all psychopathology, whether it originated in infancy, childhood, or adulthood. Whether it was a reaction to an acute traumatic episode or to chronic psychological distress depends on an individual's subjective experience. The research cited in *Trauma and Recovery*, confirms that each person's breaking point is different, "Only a small minority of exceptional people appear to be relatively invulnerable to extreme situations."[4] The issue of resiliency is so important that the entire issue of the March/April 1998 *Family Therapy Networker* was dedicated to this subject. The articles substantiated that there is a large variability of resiliency within humans, and pointed to numerous studies which indicate that there is a genetic connection which affects an individual's sensitivity, or lack of sensitivity, to vulnerability.

Because of the innate and learned differences within people, it is paramount for therapists to recognize and be acutely aware that some event which they might view as a minor happening could be emotionally devastating and traumatizing to someone. In addition, an added obstacle is that many times the person who is easily emotionally marred may find it difficult to tell anyone, including a therapist, due to feeling ashamed. Michael Basch in *Doing Brief Psychotherapy* says that shame is like a red light and tells a person to stop.[5]

If the therapeutic goal is to get the person to talk, then it is essential that a therapist does not send a message that the person should not be feeling the way he is feeling. One way to avoid sending that message is to treat every person as if he has been traumatized and to work from the trauma recovery perspective that every patient requires and needs to feel safe. The level of a patient's ability to feel secure is dependent on the construction and contents of a safe container.

Safe Container

I won't tell your secret.
That would be just telling a tale.
Instead, I will untie your knot
Without saying a word.[6]

These words written by Rumi say what every patient would hope to experience from their encounter with their therapist. However, the need for feeling safe and the desire for healing, to have their "knot" untied, cannot be assuaged with words. The initial uneasiness that every patient brings into the therapy room can only be alleviated by the presence of the therapist, who supplies the contents of a safe container.

A safe container can be imaged as the mental and emotional "stuff" which radiates from the therapist and provides an invisible protective shield around the therapeutic encounter. It may be wrapped with such things as a friendly, yet professional greeting, soft eye contact, a show of genuine interest in the person, and, as appropriate, verbal assurances.

A patient may actually feel "held" by the energy within a safe container. The effectiveness of the container is in direct proportion to the therapist's manner, integrity, sincerity, presence, and knowledge.

It is interesting that most of the qualities needed to create a safe container are not abilities that can be obtained from a book or learned in a classroom. They are skills that are developed during life experiences, interactions, and relationships. They are expressions of the characteristics, described in detail at the beginning of this chapter, which Frances Vaughan cited as psychological and spiritual healthiness: authenticity, insight, forgiveness, love, compassion, and awareness. A safe container is created from the mental, emotional, social, and spiritual maturity and well-being of the therapist.

Atmosphere

When a therapist expresses a state of physical, mental, and spiritual vitality it fills the therapy room. The opposite is also true. That is one of the primary reasons why therapists must learn how to care for themselves. The therapist is the primary "tool" or "instrument" in any psychotherapeutic encounter.

Research indicates that there is no one specific treatment, theory, or technique which is more effective than any other.[7] The primary indicators of success are the feelings that a patient has toward her therapist. The effectiveness of treatment is in direct proportion to the patient's perception of the therapist. If they like and trust the therapist and feel understood, patients experience a sense of empathy and hope, and do better in therapy than those who do not have these feelings.[8] Another study showed similar findings—therapeutic qualities, not techniques, were the deciding factors in determining the success of therapy. When therapists were well adjusted, experienced, and able to establish an empathic relationship, the patients reported successful outcomes .[9]

All of the above noted research gives increased meaning to a quote by Gandhi: "My life is my message."[10] Many people desire to help and to be of service to other members of the human race, but the desire to help is often overshadowed by the demands and requirements placed on an individual who is seen as a "healer." Before helping someone else, it is essential that the healer first learn about his own pain, his own unexpressed fears and yearnings, and deal with them.

Helen Luke described this process in an essay in *The Parabola Book of Healing*. She said,

> The feeling of wishing to save the world comes very often out of a wish to escape from having compassion on your own darkness, for what is inside yourself . . . . First comes compassion for your own weakness, and then for the person next to you.[11]

To help someone find her way out of the darkness, a therapist must know how to hold onto the light of hope. This feat can only be accomplished after the therapist has navigated his own darkest recesses and discovered a state of mind that remains stable, even though his feelings may fluctuate.

According to Lionel Corbett, "Psychological work becomes spiritual as a person realizes what it is that's been found within ourselves."[12] Certainly most mature psychotherapists set the example that healing happens from the inside out. Whether they considered psychotherapy to be spiritual work, or not, depends on their attitude toward life and consciousness.

It makes a difference when therapists are able to hold onto a larger truth and perspective as they face the darkness with their patients. When a patient is hurting, he looks for someone who is able to see beyond the face of his fear, pain, disgust, guilt, confusion, and humanness. Therapists who have worked with their own spirituality understand that beyond and within the frailty of being human lay an invisible connection to healing, to wholeness, to the all powerful Wholeness.

In *Modern Man in Search of a Soul*, Carl Jung said that "A religious attitude is an element in life whose importance can hardly be overrated."[13] He understood that the quest for psychological growth overlaps the spiritual

117

journey toward a higher consciousness. When a therapist is aware of the wondrous quality of the psyche through her own spiritual and psychological work, it is possible to bring recognition of the sacredness of psychological work to each session. The larger a therapist's perspective, the less likely it will be for her to get lost in details, and the more likely it will be for her to experience the marvelous interplay between the mental, emotional, physical, and spiritual realms.

Chapter Nine

Silent Force at Work

To be present, fully present with
someone, is a communion.

Search for Spirit

When people first learn of my profession as a psychotherapist, they frequently ask, "How do you do that?" Initially I could not even conceive of what they would be referring to. Now I know they think of the work as "listening to people's problems all day." If that was how I perceived the work, I probably couldn't do it! I am not saying that the work is always easy, but most of the time, I think of psychotherapy as interesting, challenging, and rewarding. There is the occasional patient who seems so empty it is as if he has a magnetized black hole in the center of his being that sucks in the energy of everything and everyone around them. This type of patient rarely comes to therapy of his own accord. The average patient is eagerly searching to find a different way to be in the world. What could be more exciting than to help someone find that?

Knowing that, the art of psychotherapy can still be lonely work. At times, a therapist can experience overwhelming responsibility for other people's welfare, disappointments at the appearance of set-backs and regression, and feelings of abandonment prior to a successful outcome. Even the taste of victory is not as sweet when it cannot be shared with friends and loved ones. So, who does a therapist turn to for sharing the joys, sadness, fears, and doubts of this bitter-sweet profession?

Numerous books and articles are written in professional journals that target professional "burn-out" as the serial killer of therapists. To avoid burn-out and to work through the problems encountered with transference-countertransference, it is suggested that therapists engage in their own personal therapy. Jung fostered the importance of personal therapy and explained that the benefits were far-ranging:

> We could say, without too much exaggeration, that a good half of every treatment that probes deeply consists in the [therapist's] examining himself, for only what he can put right in himself can he hope to put right in the patient. It is no loss, either, if he feels that the patient is hitting him, or scoring off him: it is his own hurt that gives the measure of his power to heal.[1]

When individuals "probe deeply," they eventually make contact with that within themselves which gives meaning to life, with their soulful nature, which Jung referred to as the Self.

Sam Keen said, "The search for spirit, for God, [for Self], is ultimately the quest to know ourselves in our heights and depths."[2] The reverse is also true. When we search our heights and depths, it is ultimately a quest to know the spirit, the God, that Self within us. Once we are familiar with this dimension of ourselves, and know that God is not only "out there" but also resides within us, we then know that we are never alone. Help is always available. As Abraham Lincoln stated, "God is the silent partner in all great enterprises."[3] This quote has always been comforting when a sense of being overwhelmed creeps into my psyche, setting off alarms and shouting about the problem in front of me being larger and more complex than my abilities.

As philosopher Alan Anderson discusses in *The Problem is God: The Selection and Care of Your Personal God*, most problems are aggravated by a person's lack of understanding regarding his beliefs about God and his relationship with God. He suggests that we must learn to trust God. To question, explore, and strive until we accept that God is at "work in any situation that concerns you; trust, not superficially, [and] not just when you can supervise God's work to make sure that he does it properly."[4] Anderson expounds on how this can take place and how we might learn to trust if we follow the advice given by Emmet Fox:

Unless we build up within our own souls a real and practical Love-consciousness, our other activities will be more or less futile. If we have the impersonal Love-consciousness [universal good will . . . plus . . . God] sufficiently well developed toward all, everything else will follow . . . . You must build up by faithful daily exercise the true Love-consciousness, and then all the rest of spiritual development will follow upon that. Love will heal you. Love will comfort you. Love will guide you. Love will illumine you.[4]

The challenge is to make spirituality a part of everyday life. It is not that anyone should feel that he needs to study for a test and have the answers—the right answers for all of life's questions—but instead, there is a need to be acutely aware of the experiences of life. To be present, fully present, with someone is a communion. In that moment, fear will dissipate and the face and feeling of Spirit, Self, God, Atman, Buddha, Christ will be known. "It" does not matter what "It" is called. "It" is always present and working within and around us. We have only to slow ourselves down and be available in the present to experience "It."

The Present

People travel halfway around the world and spend millions of dollars on books, seminars, artifacts, and potions in an attempt to obtain a sense of spirituality. I am reminded of Russell Conwell's *Acres of Diamonds*. Conwell shared that Al Halfed owned a beautiful farm, but sold it and left his family because he was driven for a desire to find diamonds. His search left him destitute, and he ended his life by throwing himself from a cliff into the sea. Meanwhile, the new owner of the farm found an unusual stone in the garden, a stone with "a strange eye of light."[5] It was a diamond. That farm is now the site of the richest diamond mines in history, the mines of Golconda, literally, acres of diamonds.

If spirituality could be equated to diamonds, people would be wise to pay attention to the story of the acres of diamonds. The truth about spirituality and sacredness is that one does not have to go to distant or even exotic places to find the spiritual and the sacred. It is found within the ground of one's daily life. There is a reminder in the Bible, ". . . the place where you are standing is holy ground." (Acts 7:33)

It is one of the paradoxes of life—that which is so special, so sacred, so spiritual is actually that which is mundane, common, and ordinary. Some exceptional books have been written to honor this precious truth: Thomas Moore's *Care of the Soul* and *The Reenchantment of Everyday Life*, Mark Epstein's *Thoughts Without a Thinker*, Lynda Sexson's *Ordinarily Sacred*, Karen Kingston's *Creating Sacred Space*, and Sam Keen's *Hymns to an Unknown God: Awakening the Spirit in Everyday Life*. These are only a few of the many that have added their voices to the wake-up call, reminding society that spirituality and sacredness are gifts of the present moment.

My husband, Ed Tuttle, wrote a book, *Raindrops in the Dust*. One of essays is "The Dawning." The opening statement is pertinent, another voice aware of spirit's call in the ordinary, everyday existence:

With sleep still trailing from my limbs, I walked the quiet morning hour through the familiar sights and smells of my home. An ordinary, every-day journey from bedroom to kitchen, a path trod

126

thousands of times in search of steaming, black coffee, some fruit or bread, to break the fast. Suddenly, in mid-stride, it was as though I was seeing it for the first time; the paintings, the books, the crumpled lap robe in Linda's favorite chair, the friendly, homely clutter, all alive in the light of the morning sun. And, as suddenly, my heart opened and my entire being thrilled to a deep and enveloping love and appreciation for this - my home.[6]

We are so inclined to seek the new, the titillating, the lure and fascination of the "yet to be." It is true, as explained by Joseph Campbell when he wrote that we stand on a street corner waiting for the light to change, totally unaware of the "sword in the stone" at our feet. The ordinary conceals the extraordinary; the familiar the mystery. There are moments like these scattered throughout our days, our lives, when we awaken briefly from our habitual sleep-walking existence to be touched by the divine.

The ordinary is saturated with the sacred calling out to souls, waiting to be noticed and appreciated. To hear the call we must quiet the clamoring voices within our minds and be fully present. Then a shift must take place, from the present time to a liminal time, "when we are between the ordinary world and the invisible one."[7] The term liminal refers to a sensory threshold, a space beyond time and place, a sacred space.

Living in a liminal space is not an easy task. Often someone is thrust into a liminal experience due to a crisis or a situation that is unknown and foreign to them. Many patients who come in search of help are in this liminal space. If a therapist is going to meet them where they are, the therapist must be familiar with a sense of liminal time. One way of cultivating liminal time is through prayerfulness.

Prayerfulness

I chose the word prayerfulness in an attempt to shift perceptions away from old concepts that view someone in prayer as a person on bended knee, with eyes closed or cast down, hands folded, and muttering words or sounds that are oft time repetitious, and all too often, meaningless. Prayerfulness is a way of being, "It is a feeling of unity . . . is accepting without being passive, is grateful without giving up. It is more willing to stand in the mystery, to tolerate ambiguity and the unknown. It honors the rightness of whatever happens."[8] Larry Dossey says that for many on-lookers prayerfulness may appear that nothing is happening, that the person engaged in prayerfulness is doing nothing. In actuality, nothing could be further from the truth; "real action is in silent moments."[9]

As Ann and Barry Ulanov explain in *Primary Speech: A Psychology of Prayer,*
Prayer starts without words and often ends without them. . . . Prayer's world is a world of honesty where we free ourselves. . . [It] is a world in which

imagination has a central role and where, as a result, the insights of those great specialists of imagination, the masters of depth psychology, are particularly useful.[10]

This type of prayer, or prayerfulness, clears an inward space to enable a therapist to tap into insights, imagination, thoughts, and feelings that are essential to clarify questions.

If a therapist has practiced, she will be able to remain totally present and yet shift to a liminal consciousness through a state of prayerfulness. Right in the midst of a confusing situation, she can move to a state of inner calm, a relaxed and receptive state, where she can make contact with core themes and inner knowledge. Prayerfulness is a state of authentic beingness, the very essence of spirituality, "where wisdom finds a special dwelling place."[11] I'm sure it is what Emerson was referring to when he said, "Let us be quiet that we may hear the whispers of the gods."[12]

When the whispers of the gods are part of a therapist's life, there is an added dimension of "magic," a wisdom that defies logic, which is present in the encounter. It is my goal to make the art of prayerfulness a constant in my life, but at this point, I am still in training. I am trying to shift from the consciousness of a human that occasionally has spiritual experiences, to the awareness that I am actually spirit having a human experience. As a therapist, there are days when I am engaged in prayerfulness, when the liminal shift occurs, and the sacred space is present. On these days there is no struggle in the midst of crises and chaos. Words flow from the deepest recesses, from a wisdom beyond conscious thought, words I would not normally use or say. At times they intrigue me, amuse me, and even shock me. Many times I am unaware of the power of what has been said. It is not until the next appointment when I am told that the patient was able to make a monumental shift, that enlightenment happened, which sprung from some "word" shared in the previous encounter. When I decorate my inner world with prayerfulness, these "ordinary" miracles happen with increasing frequency.

When major life-affirming changes occur within a life, it is like watching a fireworks display of miracles. In therapy, there have been many wonderful examples of the art work of prayerfulness. I will share two. After more than two decades of suffering from severe anxiety and panic attacks, one patient reported that "it" was gone, even trying to self-induce an attack did not work. Another patient who had lost everything she owned during six years of major depression had a stunning turn-around. She found joy in reconstructing her life, reconnecting with family, and creating new friendships.

Both of these patients had been to several other therapists prior to seeing me. At the time I was a trainee. What happened? I do not think I therapeutically "did" anything special or different. What I did was to offer many silent prayers, to believe they could overcome their problems, and that they could be healed. In sessions I attempted to establish a sense of prayerfulness, so the "whispers of the gods" might be heard in our encounters.

When coming from a place of prayerfulness, a therapist has access to a spiritual perspective that sees the Divine within each person. It is what Meister Eckhart referred to as the "spark of the soul" and what the Quakers call "the Inward Light." When a connection at that level is made, extraordinary dynamics are in play. What takes place is a willing receptivity to the Divine, "the original voice," an attitude that is best echoed in Martin Buber's observation, "The encounter with the original voice, the original source of yes or no, cannot be replaced by any self-encounter."[13]

There is a poem by Mechthikd of Magdeburg (1210-1297) that speaks to the vital process of a therapeutic encounter when prayerfulness is utilized:

> Effortlessly,
> Love flows from God into man,
> Like a bird who rivers the air
> Without moving her wings.
> Thus we move in His world
> One in body and soul,
> Though outwardly separate in form.
> As the Source strikes the note,
> Humanity sings --
> The Holy spirit is our harpist,
> And all the strings
> Which are touched in Love
> Must sound.[14]

Chapter Ten

Sacred Encounter

Intellect may allow one to walk to the
edge of soul, but one will not have the
courage to jump into the abyss of the
psyche without faith and trust.

Pivotal Relationship

It is not uncommon to hear someone say, "I would go to therapy if I thought that there was something that someone could do about my situation, but there isn't. So, why bother?" How therapy works is misunderstood by most people, those who have never gone to a therapist, and by many who have engaged in therapy. Frequently, therapists overlook and underrate the importance and the power of the therapeutic relationship. There is a tendency for therapists to give more credit to the application of theories and techniques than to the healing power of the interaction between patient and therapist.

In Murray Stein's *Transformation: Emergence of the Self,* he wrote that for years, interpretations and insights, which play a pivotal role in the healing, were thought by analysts to be the reason for their therapeutic success. Stein changed his mind after he became aware of a dramatic shift in the realization of what heals. Now, when he asks other professional psychotherapists the age-old question, "what heals in therapy?" . . . the most frequent answer [is] "the relationship." The personal relationship between the therapist and patient typically is seen as the essential factor upon which change and psychological growth depend. It is as if this is what releases the hormones that stimulate transformation in therapy.[1]

Therapy is truly a combining of energies, or as Schwartz-Salant described, it is a "strange endeavor of two people mutually constellating the unconscious."[2] This process is commonly known as transference-countertransference, and is the ever-present invisible activity that works toward or away from healing in every therapeutic session.

Jung referred to psychotherapy as "the reciprocal reaction of two psychic systems."[3] The interaction between the therapist and patient is so important that Jung said, "In any effective psychological treatment the doctor is bound to influence the patient; but this influence can only take place if the patient has a reciprocal influence on the doctor. You can exert no influence if you are not susceptible to influence. It is futile for the doctor to shield himself from the influence of the patient."[4] (Jung, 1966, p.

431) Therapist, Sheldon Kopp, said that when a special relationship develops, not only does the patient find help within the therapeutic encounter, but the therapist finds that he is also renewed and expanded. If therapy lacks the vital interaction, if all a therapist does is to advise, support, interpret, and reinforce, then the gist of the therapy is only to "teach new games, perhaps more effective games, but games, nonetheless."[5]

Productive therapy requires an inexplicable and unique relationship between the therapist and the patient, because much of what takes place in therapy occurs in the unconscious realm, in a liminal space, where it cannot be seen. The therapeutic encounter is almost impossible to evaluate or measure by any empirical method; it can only be experienced. Its effectiveness is to be determined by the people involved. In the physical world it may be impossible to decide if therapy is successful, for who can see the undercurrents that affect a patient's thoughts, feelings, perceptions, beliefs, and spiritual out-look? It is like looking at the surface of the ocean and assuming to know the depth, the hidden beauty, and the suspected terror that may lie below, beyond our vision. We might guess, but can never know unless we are submerged within it. The same is true of therapy and what takes place in the encounter between therapist and patient; no one knows unless he is involved.

Contagious Consciousness

The first step in any therapy work is to connect with the client, to establish a kinship relationship. Then, according to Michael Basch, that relationship is followed by an idealized transference. In *Doing Psychotherapy* Basch wrote that the patient must have the belief that the therapist has the "knowledge and ability to guide and support him."[6] This is one of the primary differences between a spouse or friends and a therapist. The therapist is often considered by the patient to be an idealized authority. As the therapist comes to understand the patient's needs, the therapist should acknowledge and align herself with those needs. At the same time, the therapist should not lose sight of the importance of honoring and respecting the position of being an idealized authority.

Arthur Egendorf, who wrote "Hearing People Through Their Pain," considers the mutual attunement of patient and therapist so important that he refers to it as a "communion," and says that it is "the most important antidote to traumatic estrangement."[7] Feeling estranged, abandoned, or disconnected is what drives most people to seek help. It is the therapist's job to find a way to connect and to create a "healing relationship" prior to engaging in therapeutic techniques.

Textbooks give multiple clues about greeting patients in ways that make them feel comfortable and welcome: smile, make eye contact, allow them to take the lead, be gentle, and show an interest in who they are and what they have to say. But there is so much more, because the real connection does not occur in the physical world; it takes place in the invisible. I almost did not write this book because what is really important cannot be taught, it must be experienced. My hope is that my "words become launching pads into deeper experiencing as their potential is realized."[8]

How can someone teach how to care, to love, to be compassionate, to resonate, to harmonize, and to connect with another person? Certainly not from a book or an article, classes or seminars, because these actions and attributes are the "work" of soul, and need to be learned in relationship. They require an experiential learning, such as that which happens in the therapy room. To learn the intricacies of interactions that are mental, emotional, and spiritual, one must work in the invisible and often the unconscious realm . . . areas of life which are virtually inaccessible to books and other intellectual pursuits.

Intellect may allow one to walk to the edge of soul, but one will not have the courage to jump into the abyss of the psyche without faith and trust. All too often pain and confusion stand at the edge and cry out in angry voices and actions, wanting someone to push or pull them into the underworld, the land of soul, where they must go to heal. Their cries have made them thirsty for understanding. All of this takes place in the unconscious. It is in the unconscious that the therapist can send out greetings of encouragement and support, an invitation for the person to go where the unknown lies, waiting in the darkness. Without any physical contact, the therapist's soul reaches out with invisible hands beckoning the patient, soothing, and reassuring her that she is safe in the unconscious realm, shining a light into the darkness where she must go if she is to heal.

When the patient responds at a level of soul, when she opens the door to her private and inner world, the therapist will know that her silent message of faith and hope was received. There is no doubt to those who consider their work as transpersonal that "The state of consciousness of the therapist has a far-reaching effect on the therapy process. Consciousness is seen as a field which influences, mutually interpenetrates, and provides a facilitating medium for the client's inner unfolding. . . . consciousness is contagious."[9]

Grasping, on an intellectual level, the dynamics and magnitude of how consciousness works opens a doorway to the transpersonal world of unlimited possibilities, an essential journey to wholeness. Heinz von Forster, biophysicist, cyberneticist, and mathematician says, "I have learned that we cannot understand [any] single element unless we see it as part of a magnificent whole."[10] Oyle goes on to explain Von Forster's belief that the observer and the observed are one. When we are with patients, when we observe what they are doing or saying, we are one with them. Therefore, what we think about in their presence is extremely important, possibly even more important than what we talk about.

In *Close to the Bone: Life Threatening Illness and the Search for Meaning*, Jean Shinoda Bolen reminds therapists that

> when something is expressed at a soul level, it is not something for the [therapist] to fix or minimize or deny or take personally; what is said and felt needs to be received, heard, accepted, held--as in a womb space, where insights . . . can incubate, grow, and develop fully into consciousness.[11]

The intersubjective field that exists between a therapist and patient has sometimes been referred to as a "soup" created from the interaction of the therapist and patient. It is in this soup that the miracle of healing can take place.

Some of the primary ingredients in this healing soup are love, empathy, compassion, honesty, openness, and grace. Its preparation takes time and patience, and it is heated with feelings. When ready to be enjoyed, it is served in contagious consciousness and it is a feast for everyone who is present and willing to partake in it.

Where Two and More are Gathered

There is a promise in the Bible, "If two of you agree on earth about anything they ask, it will be done for them. . . . For where two or three are gathered in my name, there I am in the midst of them." (Matthew 18:19-20) In Eastern countries when someone says that something is done in his name, it means it is done in the nature or character of the person. Therefore, the promise is that if someone meets with another person in a manner that is loving, good, uplifting, and honest, which are characteristics of the Christ consciousness, an added dimension of spiritual help will be available to produce the results desired from the meeting.

That is why the title for this section is "Where Two and More are Gathered." In a therapeutic session, when the patient is earnestly seeking help and the therapist is devoted to facilitating healing, there is always an added dimension of invisible assistance available. This factor has been noted since ancient times by various names and concepts. Jean Shinoda Bolen describes such a happening taking place:

> . . . when the eyes of the patient . . . turn inward, the room suddenly, collectively, goes silent in [a] deep way . . . the ancient Greeks would observe: 'Hermes has entered.' Hermes was the messenger god and guide of souls to the underworld. Today we say 'An Angel has come.'[12]

Whether a therapist wants to think of the unseen presence as Hermes, Jesus, Buddha, God, or angels, it does not really matter. Anyone who has had the experience, regardless of the interpretation given to it, does not doubt its validity, nor its power. It is a threshold, liminal, experience. It is a sacred, spiritual, and even mystical experience. It speaks in the voice of soul—audible and silent. Even when there are only two bodies in the room, it is obvious that other energies/presences are available.

In the *Handbook for the Soul*, Bolen describes a knowingness when soul is present:

> When people come for therapy, soul is present. When they speak to me of the experiences that have affected them deeply, trusting me with their vulnerability . . . I know that we are meeting at soul

level, that we are not just in an office but in sanctuary, and that an invisible, transpersonal healing energy enters our space. . . . I think that whenever soul is present, it's because what you're doing, whom you're with, where you are, evokes love without your thinking about it. You are totally absorbed in place or person or event, without ego, and without judgment. 13

This is sacred work. Whether someone thinks of psychology as being a spiritual practice, a humanistic endeavor, a behavioral pursuit, or just a quest into the unknown world of the unconscious, it does not really matter. A therapist, who is spiritual, even when she is not aware of her spirituality, is one who is intensely dedicated to the art of stewardship. Just as Jesus forgave the people involved in his crucifixion by saying, "Father, forgive them, for they know not what they do" (Luke 23:34), I hear a similar silent prayer being said over therapists who are committed to their work, "Bless them, even when they know not what they do."

The mystics were aware of the silent force, the third presence, in every meeting between souls. Whether one thinks of Emerson as a mystic or philosopher, he was aware of and enjoyed musing about the unseen "third force." He said,

> The action of the soul is oftener in that which is felt and left unsaid than in that which is said in any conversation . . . we are so much more. I feel the same truth so often in my trivial conversations with my neighbors that somewhat higher in each of us overlooks this play-by-play, and Jove nods to Jove from behind each of us.[14]

Jove is the god noted as the God of joy and laughter.

This thought is reminiscent of the Eastern greeting, "Namaste," meaning "the Christ within me honors the Christ within you." There have been times as a behavior analyst, while working with difficult and aggressive clients, that I have silently offered this greeting. Most often, within moments, I am aware of a physical sensation that courses through my body, and I know that our souls have met through the invitation to the third force. The energy in the room makes a shift and the client becomes calmer.

In an interview toward the end of his life, Jung was asked if he believed in God. Jung responded that he did not believe, he knew. The certainty of Jung's answer resulted from years of incessant seeking and experiencing. Early in my life, I was given a treasure that left me with the same level of certainty regarding the existence of God. When I was about five years of age I had a vision, a visitation, from a radiant lady of light. She spoke my name three times and left as elusively as she came. She has never been forgotten.

For me, there is no doubt that there is an unseen world, from which assistance and guidance are available. We can ignore "It" or work with It. It will not insist on our awareness or belief. It does not even care what we call It. It will be to us whatever we can conceive It to be. However, I am forever amused and amazed when someone is not aware of "It," this ever present force. I believe that our belief in "It" is a foundational element within the substructure of our being. Even if the belief is never verbalized, the belief in It is an essential essence that seems to radiate from and around the believer.

CHAPTER ELEVEN

SACRED WORK

The Faithkeeper is responsible for holding a higher vision, retaining faith, and being the voice of hope and inspiration when other tribe members forget.

Being Enough

Medical doctors use a variety of instruments and medications to support healing and promote curing for their patients. A psychotherapist is limited to the use of himself and the relationship with the patient as a primary healing agent. Although the therapeutic process may be aided by experience, knowledge, theory, and skillful techniques, the most important element is the capacity for the therapist to engage in a mature, non-threatening, non-judgmental relationship. As Patrick Casement pointed out in *Learning from the Patient*, a patient's most critical need is to be "in the presence of someone whose underlying attitude" is to sustain "a wish to understand [her] behavior rather than criticize it."[1] There is a desire to be understood and accepted at all levels of beingness.

One of the most beautiful descriptions of this therapeutic process, of meeting the patient at all levels of their beingness, was shared by

Carl Rogers. Naomi Remen, M.D., remembers her teacher and mentor saying,

Before every session I take a moment to remember my humanity. There is no experience that this man has that I cannot share with him, no fear that I cannot understand, no suffering that I cannot care about, because I too am human. No matter how deep his wound, he does not need to be ashamed in front of me. I too am vulnerable. And because of this, *I am enough*. Whatever his story, he no longer needs to be alone with it. This is what will allow his healing to begin.[2]

Although some therapists may not recognize it, there lives within them a hope that they will be "enough," and within that desire lies another aspiration, that they will be strong enough to be vulnerable.

In *Modern Man in Search of a Soul*, Carl Jung emphasizes the purpose for, and underlying importance of, vulnerability for therapist and patient saying,

There appears to be a conscience in mankind which severely punishes the man who does not somehow and at some time, at whatever cost to his pride, cease to defend and assert himself, and

153

instead confess himself fallible and human. Until he can do this, an impenetrable wall shuts him out from the living experience of feeling himself a man among men.[3]

A therapist is not exempt from the need to "confess," although it is not necessary to verbalize his own vulnerable experiences to a patient. Paraphrasing Ralph Waldo Emerson, "Who you are speaks so loudly, I can't hear what you're saying." If a therapist has not allowed himself to be vulnerable, he will not be able to support his client in this most important step. According to Edinger, Jung believed that "a psychotherapist can take a patient no further than he or she has gone . . . [because] the organ or instrument of psychotherapy is the personality of the psychotherapist."[4] It is with the dynamics of relationship that the soul finds the capacity to be repaired.

In the *Little Prince,* the fox explains to the prince that one's uniqueness is only known after another has taken the time and energy to care for them. The prince acknowledged that when they first met, the fox looked just like a thousand other foxes, until he befriended him. Only then did the fox's uniqueness become evident. The secret, the fox shared, is because "It is only with the heart that one can see rightly; what is essential is invisible to the eye," and "the eyes are blind. One must look with the heart." [5]

Working from this perspective, from the level of heart and soul, therapy becomes sacred work. Before engaging with a patient, to remind oneself of what is important, one might contemplate these words from Rumi: "Come, let's talk to each other through the Soul, saying things secret to the eyes and ears." [6]

Practicing Wholeness

The concept of working in the visible and invisible worlds together is not always easy. Rarely are patients privy to their therapists' spiritual affinities. Bolen cautions therapists about sharing their beliefs. She says that "revealing matters of the soul makes those who dwell in shallower waters uncomfortable."[7]

A therapist, who sees her work as psyche repair, and the patients' work as a sacred search for sanity as part of their spiritual underpinnings, must be equally devoted and attentive to her patients' physical needs and behaviors. Spirituality may be the therapist's driving force while tending to her patients' issues of addictions, abuse, joblessness, financial strife, marital and family dysfunctions, physical or mental disabilities and/or illnesses. All of these problems must be addressed and specific interventions be offered.

At the same time, a therapist would be wise to remember Emerson's words from his essay, "The Over-Soul." He wrote,

Meantime within man is the soul of the whole; the wise silence; the universal beauty, to which every part and particle is equally related; the eternal One. And this deep power in which we exist and whose beatitude is all accessible to us, is not only self-sufficing and perfect in every hour, but the act of seeing and the thing seen, the seer and the spectacle, the subject and the object, are one. We see the world piece by piece, as the sun, the moon, the animal, the tree; but the whole, of which these are the shining parts, is the soul.[8]

The very idea of a spiritual psychology rests on an acceptance of interrelated inner and outer worlds and a love and appreciation of the importance of both worlds.

Jaffe notes Jung's belief that the "outer world and God [the inner world] are two primordial experiences," equally great and both known by many names.[9] Jung adds that it is likely that the point where they meet is in psyche. Therefore, when one embraces psychology, they are automatically challenged to practice living on more than one level at the same time. The art of living in a state of wholeness requires practice. Murray Stein said,

"We practice wholeness by staying close to our true selves, [and] by using our energy to act in the world with integrity."[10] Authenticity and honesty project from therapists like a welcome mat, allowing the patients to be open, encouraging them to share their fears and confusion.

Another facet of wholeness is the idea of the therapist holding on to hope in the face of despair. It might also be described as a therapist shining the light of spirit into an area of darkness within the psyche. When considering the pros and cons about a therapist offering an attitude of hope for patients, I remembered hearing about a Native Indian tribe that appoints one of the members to the role of "Faithkeeper." The Faithkeeper is responsible for holding a higher vision, retaining faith, and being the voice of hope and inspiration when other tribe members forget.

I have personally found that many patients have dwelled in the darkness for so long that they have lost the belief in the existence of light. They have lost the belief in wholeness. Depending on the patient, it may or may not be appropriate to give voice to hope, but I think it is essential for a therapist to be a Faithkeeper. Solutions to problems do not usually lie on the paths that are familiar to the patient. One must maintain a vision of wholeness and look where the patient has failed to go.

As part of all healing, the patients must change, whether it is in the area of the physical, mental, emotional, or spiritual. They must entertain an expanded view of themselves, their lives, their beliefs, and the problem. During this process, a Faithkeeper holds a vision of unrealized potentials and possibilities. William James was being a Faithkeeper for the human race when he said,

> . . . most people live, whether physically, intellectually or morally, in a very restricted circle of their potential being. They make use of a very small portion of their possible consciousness. . . . We all have reservoirs of life to draw upon, of which we do not dream.[11]

The search for that "of which we do not dream" is the search for sanity, for wholeness.

I believe that people are looking for wholeness, and that wholeness is looking for them. To practice wholeness "in a psychological sense is to practice living on several levels at the same time. There can be no wholeness without the practical and concrete expression of life . . . in society."[12] All too often a patient comes into therapy, receives relief from a symptom, or insight into a problem, and then goes away, only to return to a similar life pattern and wonder why therapy was not successful for him. Therapy frequently stops short of individuation. The patient may have learned insights about himself and his behaviors, but failed to integrate the inner and outer worlds of his beingness. When the patient fails to connect and engage in a meaningful way with community, he has failed to complete the individuation process.

Is it possible that a therapist might be able to help a patient, even if the patient leaves therapy prematurely? If it is true that there are no boundaries to psyche, then even when someone leaves, there continues to be a connection.

Through psyche, thoughts can be carried on Hermes' silent wings and delivered to the door of a patient's mind. Knowing this as a Faithkeeper and therapist, perhaps one might send off a message to a patient with the following prose/prayer that was given to me by a friend:

> Bless your mind, that it may once again be free to dream.
>
> Bless your eyes, that they may see the beauty and the strength that is you.
>
> Bless your heart, that it may be filled with laughter and song once again.
>
> Bless your womb, that it may heal and bring forth the gift of life when you are ready.
>
> Bless your feet, which will continue to dance the dance of cycles.
>
> And, bless your spirit, which is loved and cherished.
>
> - Anonymous

Returning to Community

In every mythic story of every quest, it is necessary for the hero to return home after his journey, to share the treasure, the wealth, the boon of his successful adventure.[13] The same is true of therapeutic quests. The final step in individuation, that demonstrates psychological maturity, is when a person makes "a shift from egocentric to allocentric [concern for others] motivation"[14]

Dr. Peter Phan[15], a noted theologian, shared that the primary difference between psychology and religion lies in the phylogenetic concept of an evolutionary process, or the view of humans are monads, lacking in community responsibility and interdependency. If therapy aims only at the monadic existence of an individual and is directed only at her inner world, then it lacks half of the equation of what it means to be human. Therapy would be like packing for a trip, but not going anywhere. However, a spiritual psychological journey, one that is a sacred search for sanity, takes someone from an inner, person-centered perspective, to an interpersonal or relational position, and finally to a community and transpersonal viewpoint. Without these steps, it is not a completed journey.

Jungian analyst, Ann Belford Ulanov, writes in *The Transcendent Functioning* about the importance of not focusing on just the inner work. She shared that Jung felt that "if we sacrifice everything to the spirit [the inner world] and forget our body life, then 'this passion turns spirit into a malignant growth'."[16] Obviously, Jung never intended therapy to stop at an exploration of the inner self. Sam Keen offers some added insight regarding the process of expanding our psychological vision to include community. By looking at spirit as a verb that equates to love, there is a summons to see "a spiritual life [as a life that] is continually being expanded to include an ever-widening community."[17]

What will be required of someone who is willing to meet life in this manner? Sam Keen suggests that it "requires that we cultivate an elastic heart, an erotic body, a generous mind, and a compassionate imagination to root out whatever keeps us from loving ourselves and the others with whose lives ours are intertwined."[17] This is no small challenge for us therapists who believe that we can take our patients no further than we ourselves have gone.

There seems to be some inner drive, a craving to know, to be, and to do more, that pushes and pulls at the human heart, that wants to connect and to share, and that is willing to fight the odds to transcend beyond the fragile self. In *No Enemies Within*, a startling book about the human spirit, Donna Markova shared a pertinent quote by Patanjali:

> When you are inspired by some great purpose, some extraordinary project, all your thoughts break their bonds; your mind transcends limitations; your consciousness expands in every direction; and you find yourself in a great new and wonderful world. Dormant forces, faculties and talents become alive and you discover yourself to be a greater person by far than you ever dreamed yourself to be. [18]

With that promise held out, fears, doubts, concerns, and questions begin to fall into a new perspective. The work as a therapist, or as a patient, seems wholly worthwhile, providing the desire to reach out and share the new found treasure with others who can also prosper.

Often there is a mistaken idea that people have to do "great things" to have their lives be rewarding. I once heard that Mother Teresa said, "It's not the great things you do that matter, but the small things you do with great heart." All too often, people hold back sharing themselves with others, thinking that they are not enough, especially when they feel disconnected at the soul level.

Sometimes the person just needs to quiet the clamor from the world to hear the call of soul. There is no doubt that the soul cries out to be heard and as, biophysicist and therapist, Joan Borysenko says, "Soul, the basic substance of the universe, yearns for connection. [Once the connection is established] the interconnectedness of our souls makes service for others a natural joy."[19] Certainly, this is one of the basic premises and reasons for the effectiveness of 12-step groups.

The very act of helping people to reconnect with community, to complete their quest, is one way of "renewing [our] contract with our soul and with God."[20] In a world that all too often appears to be soul-less, we must not retreat to an inner sanctum, but instead, find ways to seed the world with spirit, with authenticity, with love, and with a "knowingness" about the true nature of self/Self. In that way, we might follow the words of the ancient sage, Plotinus: "We must close our eyes and invoke a new manner of seeing . . . A wakefulness that is the birthright of us all, though few put it to use."[21] With the new vision of our birthright, the soul is reunited and repaired, and we receive a great gift of feeling at home in this strange and fascinating existence on earth.

CHAPTER Twelve

JOURNEY INWARD AND OUTWARD

The mystery of the human race is wrapped in flesh and blood, in tears and laughter, in striving and falling and rising again, constantly evolving.

Age of Awareness

The mystery of the human race is wrapped in flesh and blood, in tears and laughter, in striving and falling and rising again, constantly evolving. The collective consciousness has reached a point where we are in the midst of a shift from an age of technology and science to a new age of consciousness, of wholeness. In the area of psychology, Jung led the way, with ideas that seemed ahead of his time. He shook the world of psychology with ideas about consciousness, collective unconsciousness, synchronicity, alchemy, the shadow, anima, animus, and so much more, including a need for the spiritual within psychology. In fact, he said, ". . . a spiritual need has produced in our time the 'discovery' of psychology."[1] The truth is that his ideas are timeless, and many people are just waking to the potential and power of Jung's insights. His work is just now "catching fire in people's imaginations."[2]

Jung was definite in his opinion that "the approach to the numinous is the real therapy and inasmuch as you attain to the numinous experiences you are released from the curse of pathology."[3] The word numinous was coined by Rudolph Otto, taking the Latin words *numen*, meaning God, and *nuere*, which is a verb for nod or beckon. Joined together in numinosum, they insinuate Divine approval.[4] Jung encouraged people to seek Divine approval, not from a God outside themselves, but from the center of their beings: "I have called this centre the self . . . . It might equally well be called the 'God within us'."[5]

This was another timeless idea of Jung's. Following is a quote from Hardy's book which supports this idea by offering passages from the Gnostic *Gospel of Thomas*,

> . . . 'if you bring forth what is within you, what you bring forth will save you. If you do not bring forth what is within you, what you do not bring forth will destroy you.' The Gnostics believed that . . . it is necessary for human beings and the human race to work through the darkness within and without in order to become truly themselves. In the Gospel of Thomas,

Jesus scorned those who thought that the Kingdom of God is in a particular place, like the heaven or the sky . . . 'the kingdom of God is inside of you and it is outside of you'.[6]

It is clear that for individuals to really know who they are, they must know the Self within them. This is the why I consider the therapeutic process a spiritual process.

Since consciousness is often symbolized by water, the metaphor of swimming seems applicable to most adult therapeutic encounters. At first someone may be afraid to get into the water, but he must get wet in order to learn how to overcome his fear and how to use the water for the enjoyment of swimming. The patient must face his fears and plunge into the depths of his being. He must dive in, to where unexpressed affect lives on, where dreams have died, and where unrealized heartfelt expectations for a safe and happy world are hiding. It is the therapist's job to help the patient to move to this place within, and to witness and support the patient as he mourns the loss of trust, innocence, hopes, dreams, and expectations. But guiding, witnessing, and supporting are not enough by themselves.

Another important element in the healing process of all psychotherapy is that the therapist does more than bear witness to pain and suffering. For patients to heal, they also need someone to witness the strength within them. The inner strength, which I am convinced is the Self, is what has made it possible for the patient to be a survivor. When this aspect is silently honored by the therapist, it is held in the realm of healing possibilities for the patient.

There are times when the therapist must encourage a client to drop the mantle of woe and move to alternative thoughts during the therapy session. One example of this happened while I was working with a middle aged man who was developmentally delayed. As a behavior specialist, I was called to help the group home staff to decrease the level of the client's temper outbursts. During the assessment, I learned that the client would become especially aggressive every other Tuesday. Checking his schedule, I learned that he went to see a psychiatrist every other Tuesday afternoon. A call to the psychiatrist revealed a clue. The patient had been seeing the doctor for the past two years. The focus of each meeting was a discussion about the death of the man's mother and how sad he has been since that time. I asked the doctor if he would try an experiment with me by changing the routine and focus of their sessions. He agreed to redirect the client's focus from the trauma of the mother's death to current day events, seeking out what was positive in the patient's life.

It took a month, two office visits, for the client to stop his aggressive behaviors. Unknowingly the doctor was feeding the client's agitation. It was as if he would cut open an old wound with each visit, never allowing it to heal. This one experience taught me that it is the therapist's job to help the client to know when it is time to move away from trauma stories and on to survivor stories.

Then, when the patient is ready to remove the cloak of victim, like changing attire, the therapist can point out the coat of the survivor, the Self, which has always been available, waiting to be noticed. When the internal image of his identity shifts, the patient will find a renewed sense of trust in himself, which will

engender hope and empowerment. These are
the some of the treasures sought in the spiritual
quest.

Spiritual Quest

When reading *Keen's Hymns to an Unknown God*, I was struck with his statement that "consciousness, compassion, and community are merely different names for the phenomenon that is the object of the spiritual quest."[7] They are fundamental characteristics of Spirit. They are also the sequential steps in the spiritual therapeutic process, and the necessary keys within the quest for Self. As stated above, the first step is to gain insight and understanding about one's consciousness. Within the exploration of consciousness lies an introduction to the Self.

This is an adventure that is a mutual journey taken on by patient and therapist. In *Doing Psychotherapy* Basch likens this process to mountain climbers, "Roped to each other, they struggle to scale the peak."[8] In their climb they are dependent on each other; "If one loses ground they both lose ground together, then regain their footing and go forward, much closer for having been in danger and helped each other out of it."[9]

Jung saw the therapist and patient as inevitably affecting each other in ways that were unexplainable, except through the "ocean of shared consciousness."[9] That is why Jung strongly recommended that all therapists should engage in ongoing therapy. He reminds those who are going to do this work that "the therapist is just as responsible for the cleanness of his own hands as the surgeon."[10]

Dawna Markova shared that her grandmother believed in healing and that healing always "began with one's mind and a kind, clean pair of hands."[11] In the Bible there is a promise that when one has "clean hands and pure heart . . . [they will] receive the blessing from the Lord." (Psalm 24:4-6) As therapists, we must do our own work to enter each session with our minds, hands, and hearts ready to be dedicated to the patient in front of us. From the clear state of consciousness will flow the next step, compassion.

Clean Heart

In *Healing Words,* Larry Dossey emphasizes the importance of love during the healing process. He reminds people in healing professions that "empathy, compassion, and love seem to form a literal bond—a resonance or 'glue'—between living things," and that "the feeling is the fuel behind the healing."[12] One of the most touching descriptions of an effective therapeutic process was told by Sheldon Kopp as he described Fritz Perls. He said that if someone was willing to work, within minutes "it was almost as though [Perls] could reach over, take hold of the zipper on your facade, and pull it down so quickly that your tortured soul would fall out onto the floor between the two of you."[13] When this type of soul surgery takes place, the patient and therapist can then work together on psyche repair, but it will never happen without the therapist's ability to be compassionate.

All people who are noted as healing presences seem to understand and to radiate these attributes. Richard Baker Roshi suggests that "we might substitute the word 'healing' for the word 'living.' Whenever we are living fully, we are in the process of healing the artificial divisions, the needless diseases, the senseless tragedies. Any account of the passionate life should include a description of the variety of the acts of love—a suggested repertoire for the complete healer.[14]

We must not underestimate the need or the transformative power of love in any relationship, especially in the therapeutic encounter.

To Pray or Not To Pray

When one considers the following words, one is likely to understand that everyone prays, whether they realize it or not. This view of prayer inspired the Ulnovs to write in *Primary Speech,*

> To pray is to listen and to hear this self who is speaking. This speech is primary because it is basic and fundamental, our ground. In prayer we say who in fact we are—not who we were, but who we are.[15]

If prayer is the act of the self talking and listening to the Self, I perceive the patient's "confessions" made to the therapist to be like a three-way call between the therapist, the patient's self, and the Self.

When one considers that the Self is always listening, then we are in prayer every time we think thoughts or sit quietly listening to the small inner voice that is often yelling from the inner reaches of our being. After much reading and thinking about this subject, I am convinced that emotion may be fuel for thoughts. Even the word emotion, when broken down, is e-motion, "e" being a symbol for energy then indicates emotion is energy-motion. Thoughts filled with energy-motion appear to have added transmitting power for communicating with the collective unconscious. Within the collective unconscious these thoughts, which all too often are thoughtless prayers, are available to all who share the collective unconscious, including patients. This one fact alone should inspire all therapists to be aware of their thoughts, and to awaken them to the concept of praying consciously, for the people they work with, for themselves, and for their work which is far reaching. This state of prayerfulness will actually be fueling the process of consciousness, compassion, and community.

Real Gold

Everyone needs time to be by himself, but there must be a balance of interaction with others to fulfill the Self-desire for wholeness. For Jung the work of individuation was incomplete without understanding the importance of the other:

> The unrelated human being lacks wholeness . . . he can achieve wholeness only through the soul, and the soul cannot exist without its other side, which is always found in a 'You.' Wholeness is a combination of I and You, these show themselves to be parts of a transcendent unity . . . [16]

The world is in need of those who have made the spiritual quest of traveling between their inner and outer worlds, of those who have made the connection with Self, and know there is something bigger than the individual self. It does not matter what name they have given to it. What matters is to know that there is something that supports, nourishes, and guides individuals in their search for wholeness.

At times the inner journey is frustratingly difficult, excruciatingly painful, and seemingly never-ending, which is why the therapist must be able to hold on to the knowing that the quest is truly worthwhile. The therapist must encourage, reassure, and provide hope for her patients when they are too discouraged to go on. When a therapist has made her own journey, she knows that there is gold within the depths, enough for one's self and to share.

The more someone finds within herself, the more she will have to share, which makes a better world for all. The value of the quest should not be undervalued, for as Jung pointed out, ". . . the value of a community depends on the spiritual and moral stature of the individuals composing it."[17]   We can become a stronger community as we learn more about the depths and heights of the experience of being human. The following prose by Pierre Teilhard de Chardin offers up the essence of why I wrote this paper:

> But if . . . man sees a new door opening above him, a new stage for his development; if each of us can believe that he is working so that the Universe may be raised, in him and through him, to higher

level—then a new spring of energy will well forth in the heart of Earth's workers. The whole great human organism, overcoming a momentary hesitation, will draw its breath and press on with strength renewed.[18]

No one has to really "do" anything to repair the soul. Healing is a transpersonal experience that takes place beyond space and time. It frequently happens within the safe therapeutic relationship, when patients find that part of themselves that is willing to trust another person. During the process, they explore the areas of their "inner home" where their life spirit dwells. They find and examine the aspects of self that feel damaged, broken, or incomplete.

This cleansing process, this care of the soul leads a patient to discover that each part, even the broken and damaged parts, is important and adds character. It is a delight as a therapist to watch a patient find that within the dust and dirt of the neglected past there are unexpected and valuable treasures. Such is the work and the privilege of being a practitioner of psychotherapy, which I prefer to think of as psyche repair. This affectionate term is used to remind myself of my mission in life, which is also expressed in the motto of my alma mater, Pacifica Graduate Institute. Psyche repair is the art of "tending the care of soul in the world."

End Notes

ACKNOWLEDGEMENTS
1. Upanishads. (1965). (J. Mascaro, Trans.). The Upanishads: Translations from the Sanskrit. London: Peguin.

INTRODUCTION - OFF-LIMITS
1. Edinger, E. (1997). The vocation of depth psychotherapy. Psychological Perspectives: A Journal of Global Consciousness Integrating Psyche, Soul, and Nature, 35, 8-22, p 10.

CHAPTER ONE – OVERVIEW
Psychotherapy: Sacred or Profane?
1. Merriam-Webster's collegiate dictionary (10th ed.). (1993). Springfield, MA: Merriam-Webster.
2. Talbot, M. (1991). Holographic universe. New York: Harper Collins.
3. Emerson, R. W. (1951). Emerson's essays. New York: Harper & Row, p 1.
4. Cortright, B. (1997). Psychotherapy and spirit: Theory and practice in transpersonal psychotherapy. Albany, NY: State University of New York Press, p. 81.

Evolution of Psyche
5. Revised Standard Version (RSV). In Layman's parallel bible. (1973). Grand Rapids, MI: Zondervan.

6. Gottlieb, A. (1997, February). Crisis of consciousness. <u>UNTE Reader</u> . Minneapolis, MN: Lens Publication, p. 48.
7. Corbett, L. (1996). <u>The religious function of the psyche</u>. New York: Rutledge. Corbett, L. (1996). <u>The religious function of the psyche</u>. New York: Rutledge, p. 67.

Many Faces of Love

8. Kelsey, M. T. (1973). Modern Christianity and healing. <u>In healing and Christianity in ancient thought and modern times</u> (pp. 200-242). New York: Harper and Row.
9. Dossey, L. (1993). <u>Healing words: The power of prayer and the practice of medicine</u>. New York: Harper Collins, p. 17
10. Carlson, R. & Shield, B. (Eds.) (1989). <u>Healers on healing</u>. Los Angeles: Jeremy P. Tarcher.
11. Fleishman, P. (1989). <u>The healing zone: Religious issues in psychotherapy</u>. New York: Paragon House, pp. 209-210.

Mutual Blessing

12. Stein, M. (1996). <u>Practicing wholeness: Analytical psychology and Jungian thought</u>.. New York: Chiron, p.103.
13. Stein, M. (1996). <u>Practicing wholeness: Analytical psychology and Jungian thought</u>.. New York: Chiron, p. 69.

Invitation to Wholeness

14. Ulanov, A. B. (1996). The functioning transcendent: A study in analytical psychology. Wilmette, IL: Chiron, p ix.

15. Jung, C.G. (1978). The structure and dynamics of the psyche. In The collected works of C.G. Jung, (Vol. 16). Princeton, NJ: Princeton University Press, p. 357.

16. Hardy, J. (1987). A psychology with a soul: Psychosynthesis in evolutionary context. New York: Routledge & Kegan Paul, p. 113.

17. Richards, P. S. & Bergin, A. E. (1997). A spiritual strategy for counseling and psychotherapy. Washington D. C.: American Psychological Association, p. 5.

18. Collier, R. (1976). Riches within your reach: The law of the higher potential. Ramesy, N. J.: Robert Collier Book, p. 6.

CHAPTER TWO - DEEP CALLS UNTO DEEP
Give Me Meaning

1. Carlson, R. & Shield, B. (Eds.) (1995). Handbook for the soul. Boston: Little, Brown, p.45.

What's In a Name?

2. Jung, C.G. (1933). Modern man in search of a soul. (W. S. Dell & C. F. Baynes, Trans.). New York: Harcourt, Brace, & World.

186

3. Jung, C. G. (1971). <u>The portable Jung</u>. (R. F. C. Hull, Trans.). New York: Viking Press.
4. Jaffe, L. W. (1990). <u>Liberating the heart: Spirituality and Jungian psychology</u>. Toronto, Canada: Inner City Books.
5. Jung, C.G. (1965). <u>Memories, dreams, reflections</u>. (R. & C. Winston, Trans.). New York: Vintage Books, p.45
6. Jaffe, L. W. (1990). <u>Liberating the heart: Spirituality and Jungian psychology</u>. Toronto, Canada: Inner City Books, p. 70.

Sacred Search

7. Frankl, V. (1963). <u>Man's search for meaning: An introduction to logotherapy</u>. (I. Lasch, Trans.). New York: Pocket Books,
8. Cortright, B. (1997). <u>Psychotherapy and spirit: Theory and practice in transpersonal psychotherapy</u>. Albany, NY: State University of New York Press.
9. Keen, S. (1994). <u>Hymns to an unknown God</u>. New York: Bantam Book, p. xxiii.
10.Jung, C.G. (1965). <u>Memories, dreams, reflections</u>. (R. & C. Winston, Trans.). New York: Vintage Books, p. 82.
11.Carlson, R. & Shield, B. (Eds.) (1995). <u>Handbook for the soul</u>. Boston: Little, Brown, p. 32.

187

12.Anderson, D. & Worthen, D. (1997). Exploring a fourth dimension: Spirituality as a resource for the couple therapist. <u>Journal of Marital and Family Therapy</u>. PsychLit, IS: 0194-472X, p. 97.

Spirit's Child

13.Remen, R.N. (1991). Spirit: Resource for healing. In <u>Noetic Sciences Collection: 1980 to 1990 ten years of consciousness research</u>. Sausalito, CA: Institute of Noetic Sciences, p. 63.

14.Corbett, L. (1996). <u>The religious function of the psyche</u>. New York: Rutledge, p. 122.

15.Ulanov, A. B. (1996). <u>The functioning transcendent: A study in analytical psychology</u>. Wilmette, IL: Chiron, p. 186.

16.Carlson, R. & Shield, B. (Eds.) (1995). <u>Handbook for the soul</u>. Boston: Little, Brown, p. 108.

17.American Psychiatric Association. (1994). <u>Diagnostic and statistical manual of mental disorders</u>. (4th ed.). Washington, DC: Author.

18.Wilmer, H. A. (1987). <u>Practical Jung: Nuts and bolts of Jungian psychotherapy</u>. Wilmette, IL: Chiron, p. 112.

19. Remen, R.N. (1991). Spirit: Resource for healing. In Noetic Sciences Collection: 1980 to 1990 ten years of consciousness research. Sausalito, CA: Institute of Noetic Sciences, p. 62.

CHAPTER THREE - WHOLENESS REVOLUTION

Consciousness Evolution

1. Meier, C.A. (1989). Healing, dream, and ritual. Einsiedeln, Switzerland: Daimon Verlag.

2. Jung, C.G. (1965). Memories, dreams, reflections. (R. & C. Winston, Trans.). New York: Vintage Books, p. 333.

3. Jung, C.G. (1965). Memories, dreams, reflections. (R. & C. Winston, Trans.). New York: Vintage Books, p. 256.

4. Hansen, M. V. & Nichols, B. (1996). Out of the blue: Delight comes into our lives. New York: Harper Collins.

5. Jaffe, L. W. (1990). Liberating the heart: Spirituality and Jungian psychology. Toronto, Canada: Inner City Books, p. 23.

6. Jaffe, L. W. (1990). Liberating the heart: Spirituality and Jungian psychology. Toronto, Canada: Inner City Books, p. 19.

7. Holmes, E. (1970). The power of belief. Los Angeles: Science of Mind Publication, p. 21

Warfare to Romance
8. Cortright, B. (1997). <u>Psychotherapy and spirit: Theory and practice in transpersonal psychotherapy</u>. Albany, NY: State University of New York Press, p. 210.
9. Keen, S. (1994). <u>Hymns to an unknown God</u>. New York: Bantam Book, p. xxi.
10. Tennyson, A. (1936) In <u>The best loved poems of the American people</u>. (H. Felleman, Ed.). Garden City, NY: Doubleday, p. 572.

CHAPTER FOUR – NO BOUNDARIES
Universal Force
1. Oyle, I. (1979). <u>The healing word</u>. Milbrae, CA: Celestial Arts, p. 36.
2. Marrone, R. (1990). <u>Body of knowledge: An introduction to body/mind psychology</u>. Albany, NY: State University of New York Press, p. 146.

Seemless Reality
3. Talbot, M. (1991). <u>Holographic universe</u>. New York: Harper Collins, p. 48.
4. Talbot, M. (1991). <u>Holographic universe</u>. New York: Harper Collins, pp.60-61.
5. 5. Hardy, J. (1987). <u>A psychology with a soul: Psychosynthesis in evolutionary context</u>. New York: Routledge & Kegan Paul, p. 110.

6. Holmes, E. (1970). The power of belief. Los Angeles: Science of Mind Publication, p. 95.

Outburst of Soul

7. Keen, S. (1994). Hymns to an unknown God. New York: Bantam Book, p. xv.
8. Jung, C.G. (1965). Memories, dreams, reflections. (R. & C. Winston, Trans.). New York: Vintage Books, p. 339.
9. Markova, D. (1994). No enemies within. Emeryville, CA: Conari Press, p. 44.

Soul Force

10. Carlson, R. & Shield, B. (Eds.) (1995). Handbook for the soul. Boston: Little, Brown, p.164.
11. Sardello, R. (1992). Facing the world with soul: The reimagination of modern life. Hudson, NY: Harper Perennial, p. xv.
12. Cortright, B. (1997). Psychotherapy and spirit: Theory and practice in transpersonal psychotherapy. Albany, NY: State University of New York Press, p. 239.
13. Von-Franz, M. (1993). Psychotherapy. Boston, Shambhala, pp. 244-245.

CHAPTER FIVE – SEEDS OF LOVE
Unconscious Connection

1. Holmes, E. (1970). The power of belief. Los Angeles: Science of Mind Publication, p. 77.

2. Dossey, L. (1993). <u>Healing words: The power of prayer and the practice of medicine</u>. New York: Harper Collins.

3. Emerson, R. W. (1951). <u>Emerson's essays</u>. New York: Harper & Row, p. 56.

4. Hansen, M. V. & Nichols, B. (1996). <u>Out of the blue: Delight comes into our lives</u>. New York: Harper Collins, p. 3.

5. Dossey, L. (1993). <u>Healing words: The power of prayer and the practice of medicine</u>. New York: Harper Collins, p. xvii.

6. Dossey, L. (1993). <u>Healing words: The power of prayer and the practice of medicine</u>. New York: Harper Collins, p. xix.

Healing – Not Curing

7. Heiler, F. (1990). The essence of prayer. In <u>The world treasury of modern religious thought</u> (J. Pelikan, Ed.). Boston: Little, Brown, p. 310.

8. Jung, C. G. (1971). <u>The portable Jung</u>. (R. F. C. Hull, Trans.). New York: Viking Press, p. 277.

9. Beane, W.C. (March/April 1998). Curing and healing: Not always the same. <u>Venture Inward, 14</u>, 12-13, p. 12.

10. Remen, R.N. (1991). Spirit: Resource for healing. In <u>Noetic Sciences Collection: 1980 to 1990 ten years of consciousness research</u>. Sausalito, CA: Institute of Noetic Sciences, p. 62.

CHAPTER SIX – TENDING THE CARE OF THE SOUL

Finding a pathway to Healing

1. Herman, J. (1997). <u>Trauma and recovery</u>. New York: Harper Collins.

Working in the Invisible Realm

2. Cortright, B. (1997). <u>Psychotherapy and spirit: Theory and practice in transpersonal psychotherapy</u>. Albany, NY: State University of New York Press, p. 156.

3. Vaughan, F. (1991). Spiritual issues in psychotherapy. <u>Journal of Transpersonal Psychology</u>, (2), 105-120, p. 107.

A Path with a Heart

4. Kasl, C.S. (1997). <u>A home for the heart</u>. New York: Harper Collins, p. 3.

5. Kasl, C.S. (1997). <u>A home for the heart</u>. New York: Harper Collins, p. 3.

6. Rumi, M. J. (1993). (N. Ergin, Trans.) <u>Magnificent one: Selected verses from Divan-I Kebir</u>. Burdett, NY: Larson, p. 15.

CHAPTER SEVEN – SACRED SPACE
Something Special
Something About This Place

1. Keen, S. (1994). <u>Hymns to an unknown God</u>. New York: Bantam Book, p. xxii.
2. Vaughan, F. (1991). Spiritual issues in psychotherapy. <u>Journal of Transpersonal Psychology</u>,(2), 105-120, pp. 117-118.

Sacred Place

3. <u>Merriam-Webster's collegiate dictionary</u> (10th ed.). (1993). Springfield, MA: Merriam-Webster, p. 917.
4. Kingston, K. (1997). <u>Creating sacred space with feng shui</u>. New York: Broadway Books, p. 11.
5. Kingston, K. (1997). <u>Creating sacred space with feng shui</u>. New York: Broadway Books, p. 39.

CHAPTER EIGHT – A SAFE PLACE
Connection

1. Moore, T. (1992). <u>Care of the soul</u>. New York: Harper Collins, pp. 19-20.
2. Herman, J. (1997). <u>Trauma and recovery</u>. New York: Harper Collins, p. 61.
3. Herman, J. (1997). <u>Trauma and recovery</u>. New York: Harper Collins, p. 160.
4. Herman, J. (1997). <u>Trauma and recovery</u>. New York: Harper Collins, p.58.

5. Basch, M. F. (1995). Doing brief psychotherapy. New York: Basic Books, pp.77-98.

Contents

6. Rumi, M. J. (1993). (N. Ergin, Trans.) Magnificent one: Selected verses from Divan-I Kebir. Burdett, NY: Larson, p. 15.

Atmosphere

7. Stiles, W. B., Shapiro, D. A., & Elliot, R. (1986). Are all psychotherapies equivalent? American Psychologist, 41, pp. 165-180.

8. Strupp, H. H. (1986). Psychotherapy: Research, practice, and public policy. American Psychologist, 41, pp. 120-130.

9. Strupp, H.H. & Binder, J.L. (1984). A guide to time-limited psychotherapy. New York: Basic Books.

10. Vaughan, F. (1991). Spiritual issues in psychotherapy. Journal of Transpersonal Psychology,(2), 105-120.

11. Luke, H. (1994). An interview with Helen Luke. In The parabola book of healing (pp. 211-218). New York: Continuum, p. 216.

12. Corbett, L. (1996). The religious function of the psyche. New York: Rutledge, p. 3.

13.Jung, C.G. (1933). Modern man in search of a soul. (W. S. Dell & C. F. Baynes, Trans.). New York: Harcourt, Brace, & World, p. 67.

CHAPTER NINE – A SILENT FORCE AT WORK
Search for Spirit
1. Jung, C. G. (1951) Fundamental questions of psychotherapy. In The collected works of C. G. Jung, (Vol 16). Princeton, NJ: Princeton University Press, p. 116.
2. Keen, S. (1994). Hymns to an unknown God. New York: Bantam Book, p. xxiii.
3. Greenberg, S. (Ed.) (1971). Treasury of the art of living. North Hollywood, CA: Wilshire Book.
4. Anderson, A. (1984). The problem is God: The selection and care of your personal God. Walpoint, NH: Stillpoint, p. 192.

The Present
5. Conwell, R. H. (1921). Acres of diamonds. Marina del Rey, CA: DeVorss, p. 6.
6. Tuttle, E. V. (2003) Raindrops in the dust: Dreams, memories and reflections. Santa Maria, CA: Pathways of Lights, p. 23.
7. Bolen, J. S. (1996). Close to the bone: Life threatening illness and the search for meaning. New York: Scribner, p. 19

Prayerfulness

8. Dossey, L. (1993). <u>Healing words: The power of prayer and the practice of medicine</u>. New York: Harper Collins, p. 24.

9. Emerson, R. W. (1951). <u>Emerson's essays</u>. New York: Harper & Row, p. 116.

10. Ulanov, A. & Ulanov, B. (1982). <u>Primary speech: A psychology of prayer</u>. Atlanta, GA: John Knox, p. vii.

11. Ulanov, A. & Ulanov, B. (1982). <u>Primary speech: A psychology of prayer</u>. Atlanta, GA: John Knox, p. ix.

12. Greenberg, S. (Ed.) (1971). <u>Treasury of the art of living</u>. North Hollywood, CA: Wilshire Book, p. 108

13. Buber, M. (1952). <u>Eclipse of God: Studies in the relation between religion and psychology</u>. New York: Harper, 18.

14. Mitchell, S. (Ed.) (1989). <u>The enlightened heart: An anthology of sacred poetry</u>. New York: Harper and Row, p.65.

CHAPTER TEN – SACRED ENCOUNTER
Pivotal Relationship

1. Stein, M. (1998b). <u>Transformation: Emergence of the self</u>. College Station, TX: Open Court, p. 73

2. Schwartz-Salant, N. (1984). Archetypal factors underlying sexual acting out in transference-countertransference process, Chiron, 1-30, p. 29.
3. Jung, C. G. (1935). The principles of practical psychotherapy. In The collected works of C. G. Jung, (Vol 16). Princeton, NJ: Princeton University Press, p. 4.
4. Jung, C. G. (1966) Problems in modern psychotherapy. In The collected works of C. G. Jung, (Vol 16). Princeton, NJ: Princeton University Press, p. 431.

Continuous Consciousness

5. Kopp, S.B. (1971). Guru: Metaphors from a psychotherapist. Palo Alto, CA: Science and Behavior Books, p. 178.
6. Basch, M. F. (1980). Doing psychotherapy. New York: Basic Books, p. 19.
7. Egendorf, A. (1995). Hearing people through their pain. Journal of Traumatic Stress, 8. (1), 5-28, p. 23.
8. Cortright, B. (1997). Psychotherapy and spirit: Theory and practice in transpersonal psychotherapy. Albany, NY: State University of New York Press, p. 239.
9. Cortright, B. (1997). Psychotherapy and spirit: Theory and practice in transpersonal psychotherapy. Albany, NY: State University of New York Press, p. 57.

10. Oyle, I. (1979). <u>The healing word</u>. Milbrae, CA: Celestial Arts, p. 96..

11. Bolen, J. S. (1996). <u>Close to the bone: Life threatening illness and the search for meaning</u>. New York: Scribner, p. 18.

Where Two or More are Gathered

12. Bolen, J. S. (1996). <u>Close to the bone: Life threatening illness and the search for meaning</u>. New York: Scribner, p. 13.

13. Carlson, R. & Shield, B. (Eds.) (1995). <u>Handbook for the soul</u>. Boston: Little, Brown, pp. 4-5.

14. Emerson, R. W. (1951). <u>Emerson's essays</u>. New York: Harper & Row, p. 197.

CHAPTER ELEVEN - SACRED WORK
Being Enough

1. Casement, P. J. (1991). <u>Learning from the patient</u>. New York: Guilford, p. 314.

2. Remen, R. N. (1997, July). Listening: A powerful tool for healing. <u>Science of Mind, 70</u> (7), 14-19, pp. 16-17.

3. Jung, C.G. (1933). <u>Modern man in search of a soul</u>. (W. S. Dell & C. F. Baynes, Trans.). New York: Harcourt, Brace, & World, pp. 34-35.

4. Edinger, E. (1997). The vocation of depth psychotherapy. <u>Psychological Perspectives: A Journal of Global Consciousness Integrating Psyche, Soul, and Nature, 35</u>, 8-22, p 21.

5. Saint Exupery, A. (1971). <u>The little prince</u>. (K. Woods, Trans.) New York: Harvest/HBJ Book. (originally published in 1943), p. 87.

6. Rumi, M. J. (1993). (N. Ergin, Trans.) <u>Magnificent one: Selected verses from Divan-I Kebir</u>. Burdett, NY: Larson, p. 11.

Practicing Wholeness

7. Bolen, J. S. (1996). <u>Close to the bone: Life threatening illness and the search for meaning</u>. New York: Scribner, p. 18.

8. Emerson, R. W. (1951). <u>Emerson's essays</u>. New York: Harper & Row, p. 190.

9. Jaffe, L. W. (1990). <u>Liberating the heart: Spirituality and Jungian psychology</u>. Toronto, Canada: Inner City Books, p. 31.

10. Stein, M. (1998a). <u>Jung's map of the soul</u>. Chicago, IL: Open Court.

11. Walsh, R. N. & Vaughan, F. (1980). <u>Beyond ego: Transpersonal dimensions in psychology</u>. Los Angeles: Jeremy P. Tarcher, p. 1.

12. Stein, M. (1996). <u>Practicing wholeness: Analytical psychology and Jungian thought</u>.. New York: Chiron, p. 12.

Returning to Community

13. Campbell, J. (1968). <u>The hero with a thousand faces</u>. Princeton, NJ: Princeton University Press, p. 30.

14. Walsh, R. N. & Vaughan, F. (1980). Beyond ego: Transpersonal dimensions in psychology. Los Angeles: Jeremy P. Tarcher, p. 5.

15. Phan, P. (1997, June). Christian theology and psychotherapy in partnership. Unpublished lecture presented at Pacifica Graduate Institute, Carpinteria, CA.

16. Ulanov, A. B. (1996). The functioning transcendent: A study in analytical psychology. Wilmette, IL: Chiron, p. 20.

17. Keen, S. (1994). Hymns to an unknown God. New York: Bantam Book, p. 229.

18. Markova, D. (1994). No enemies within. Emeryville, CA: Conari Press, p. 320.

19. Carlson, R. & Shield, B. (Eds.) (1995). Handbook for the soul. Boston: Little, Brown, p. 47.

20. Carlson, R. & Shield, B. (Eds.) (1995). Handbook for the soul. Boston: Little, Brown, p. 106.

21. Plotinus, (1964). The essential Plotinus. (E. O. Brien, Transl.) Indianapolis: Hackett.

CHAPTER TWELVE – JOURNEY INWARD AND OUTWARD

A New Age of Awareness

1. Jung, C. G. (1971). The portable Jung. (R. F. C. Hull, Trans.). New York: Viking Press, p. 462.

2. Cameron, J. (1996). <u>The vein of gold: A journey to your creative heart</u>. New York: Putman Book, p. 288.
3. Walsh, R. N. & Vaughan, F. (1980). <u>Beyond ego: Transpersonal dimensions in psychology</u>. Los Angeles: Jeremy P. Tarcher, p. 48.
4. Corbett, L. (1996). <u>The religious function of the psyche</u>. New York: Rutledge.
5. Jung, C. G. (1966) Problems in modern psychotherapy. In <u>The collected works of C. G. Jung</u>, (Vol 16). Princeton, NJ: Princeton University Press, p. 238.
6. Hardy, J. (1987). <u>A psychology with a soul: Psychosynthesis in evolutionary context</u>. New York: Routledge & Kegan Paul, p. 130.

Spiritual Quest

7. Keen, S. (1994). <u>Hymns to an unknown God</u>. New York: Bantam Book, p. 231.
8. Basch, M. F. (1980). <u>Doing psychotherapy</u>. New York: Basic Booksp. 31.
9. Cameron, J. (1996). <u>The vein of gold: A journey to your creative heart</u>. New York: Putman Book, p. 289.

10. Jung, C. G. (1914). Some crucial points in psychoanalysis: A correspondence between Dr. Jung and Dr. Loy. In The collected works of C. G. Jung, (Vol 4). Princeton, NJ: Princeton University Press, 260.
11. Markova, D. (1994). No enemies within. Emeryville, CA: Conari Press, p. 227.

With a Clean Heart

12. Dossey, L. (1993). Healing words: The power of prayer and the practice of medicine. New York: Harper Collins, p. 111.
13. Kopp, S.B. (1971). Guru: Metaphors from a psychotherapist. Palo Alto, CA: Science and Behavior Books, p. 146.
14. Keen, S. (1983). The passionate life: Stages of loving. New York: HarperCollins, p. 209.
15. Ulanov, A. & Ulanov, B. (1982). Primary speech: A psychology of prayer. Atlanta, GA: John Knox, p. 1.

An Open Door

16. Stein, M. (1996). Practicing wholeness: Analytical psychology and Jungian thought.. New York: Chiron, p. 7.
17. Jung, C. G. (1970) The undiscovered self: Present and future. In The collected works of C. G. Jung, (Vol 10). Princeton, NJ: Princeton University Press, p. 303.

18.Dyer, W. W. (1995). <u>Your sacred self:</u> <u>Making the decision to be free</u>. New York: Harper Collins, p. 313.

INDEX

206

209

About the Author

During this "parenthesis in eternity" known as my life, I've never been a world traveler, but I am an adventurer, exploring the essence of life. I've scaled to exhilarating and victorious peaks and crawled for times in the darkest depths, stuck in the muck and mire of pain, exhaustion, and hopelessness. Somehow, through it all, a part of me always knew the truth, that I am a light bearer. Interesting that as an adult, I readopted my maiden name, Bearer. A "bearer" is one who carries, holds, and delivers. I hope I will always live up to the commitment of being a Bearer of all that is good and worthwhile in life.

After the God of my childhood died, I spent years in denial, Self-denial. I wrapped the cloak of atheist and agnostic around my soul. In my thirties I recognized that the death of God as a being allowed a transition to occur, and when God resurrected into my life He, She, It, was a God of Spirit—everywhere—in, out, and around all people, places and things.

Fate was once again actively at work in my life.   I met my husband, a New Thought minister, and began the process of trading my agnostic cloak for ministerial robes. My robe is more like Jacob's many colored coat. It has patches of child, parent, employee, volunteer, earth-mother, manager, public speaker, gypsy, grandparent, student, therapist, educator, friend, lover, and wife. Now there will be another patch as author.   With age, I have an ever growing appreciation for my precious coat and realize it has been sewn together with the needle of spirit and the threads of love.